THE STORY ROAD
TO LITERACY

THE STORY ROAD TO LITERACY

Rita Roth

Library of Congress Cataloging-in-Publication Data

Roth, Rita.
    The story road to literacy / by Rita Roth.
      p. cm.
    Includes bibliographical references and index.
    ISBN 1-59158-323-3 (pbk. : alk. paper)
    1. Language arts—United States. 2. English language—
Study and teaching—Foreign speakers. 3. Children of
immigrants—Education—United States. 4. Tales—Study and
teaching—United States. I. Title.
  LB1576.R754 2006
  372.6—dc22   2005030835

British Library Cataloguing in Publication Data is available.

Library of Congress Catalog Card Number: 2005030835
ISBN: 1-59158-323-3

First published in 2006

Libraries Unlimited/Teacher Ideas Press, 88 Post Road West, Westport, CT 06881
A Member of the Greenwood Publishing Group, Inc.
www.lu.com

Printed in the United States of America

The paper used in this book complies with the
Permanent Paper Standard issued by the National
Information Standards Organization (Z39.48–1984).

10 9 8 7 6 5 4 3 2 1

For teachers—our guides

on the road to literacy.

CONTENTS

FOREWORD

I met Rita many years ago when she was a first grade teacher in a suburb of St. Louis, Missouri. I was working at her school along with several other Washington University teacher education faculty, in a program called "STEP", the acronym for Washington University's School-based Teacher Education Program headquartered in the basement of her school.

Stories of Rita's teaching prowess preceded her. I had heard from a colleague about her famous "Chicken Soup with Rice" unit and went to observe. This classic children's book by Maurice Sendak served as a theme for a year-long unit that integrated virtually all school subjects, from reading, writing, and arithmetic to visual arts, music, science, consumer economics, nutrition education and social studies. I returned frequently to observe an amazingly wide array of active learning experiences that provided opportunities for students to master the basics while expanding and deepening their intellectual and aesthetic abilities and interests. The class prepared chicken soup with rice from scratch, hatched chicks and delivered them to a farm where the class slept overnight in a barn. All this clearly required many hours of careful teacher preparation, a classroom richly provisioned with books, cultural and natural artifacts, plants, and small animals. But what stands in relief in my memory is the atmosphere which was evident from the moment I entered her classroom reflecting Rita's abiding affection for children, and her respect for their knowledge and ways of thinking, as well as their questions and curiosities about the world around them and the wider social world.

This book is a product of Rita Roth's career and her commitment to the principles and practices of democratic, progressive education as a teacher and teacher of teachers. It provides teachers and others who work with children with a way of thinking about and a pedagogy for teaching children to read, write, speak, and develop their critical faculties while promoting compassion and understanding of self, one's own culture, and the culture of others. The book arrives in perilous times for the future of democracy and public education in America. The tradition of democratic, progressive pedagogy is under attack by testing policies of the federal and many state governments that have the effect of narrowing the curriculum and greatly restricting the autonomy of local communities, teachers and parents. The No Child Left Behind Act puts in the hands of state and federal government unprecedented control of what is taught and how to teach. Resistance to these policies is growing and this book is testimony to the fact that the tradition of progressive, multicultural education is alive and well.

Harold Berlak
Oakland, California, 2005

ACKNOWLEDGMENTS

My sincere thanks go to friends, colleagues, and family for their encouragement.

I will always treasure knowing the students whose stories grace this book. I am grateful to the teachers who believed in the usefulness of this book and welcomed me into their schools: Jerri Johnson, Julie Badders, Nancy Allen, Teresa Davidson, and Judy Kings-Knorr. To teachers who field-tested materials, I thank Susan Gittinger, Kathy Quinn, Alivia Danilson, Michelle Garrett, and Lisa Ramey.

I am grateful for the unending patience of Terry Forge who cheerfully provided answers to my computer dilemmas. I thank my daughter, Beth Levant, who was always there to guide me through bibliographies and references.

A special thank you to Norman Burkart for his invaluable technical help.

I am indebted to my dear friends and teachers, Harold and Ann Berlak, for awakening me to the challenges and joys of inquiry into issues of schooling and literacy.

To my husband—a constant source of support—I am eternally grateful.

INTRODUCTION

Yegor's Story

Once there was a forest. And in this forest there lived different kinds of animals. The king of this place is a lion, you know. Once he goes to hunt.

This lion is very kind to every animal. He doesn't eat healthy animals. He eats sick ones that are going to die. So, he looks and he couldn't find anything. Then he finds a fox, you know, and he chases him and when he is ready to eat him, the fox says, "Don't eat me!" and those kinds of stuff. You know, a fox is kind of tricky. So, he says, "Okay."

So, he tells the fox to come and live with him. So, when the lion catches something to eat, he brings it to table and they both eat. So, once when this lion goes hunting, somebody shoots this lion. When he comes home, you know, he asks for water from the fox. The fox took a big stone and throws it at the lion.

The lion says, "Why did you do this to me? I've been always good to you."

The fox says, "First when you come, you say, 'I have to kill you.' Now, I have to kill YOU."

So, he kills the lion.

The meaning of this story is that in the world it's some people, you know, that even if you are some kind of kindness to them and everything, they will be bad to you.

You can't trust some people.

Twelve-year-old Yegor recently immigrated to the United States from Azerbaijan. His story illustrates the meaningful role folktales can play in our lives. The story contains traditional characteristics of folktales—the conversational tone typical of the oral tradition, the brevity and simplicity of style, and the use of animals to portray human traits. It also reveals what, for Yegor, must have been a carefully learned lesson that he shares through a story—"You can't trust some people."

Story has power that never ceases to impress. The persistence of ancient stories attests to its endurance. For example, in the sixth century

BC, the Greek slave, Aesop, told tales that kept his master out of trouble. These are the tales that continue to entertain us today. Consider the universality of *story*—virtually every culture calls upon the power of story to perpetuate its values, values that are remarkably similar. We see this in the hundreds of variations of common story types and motifs found in cultures separated by geography, language, and custom. Although the variants reflect their cultural settings, they fall into similar categories or motifs. For example, there are well over seven hundred variants of the Cinderella motif throughout the world.[1] Cultures as distinct as Native American, Vietnamese, Chinese, or Korean, as well as Western European—to mention a few—all evidence stories that, while distinct in many ways, still fit the Cinderella motif.

The impact of *story* remains impressive, whether in the ancient voice of an Aesop or the modern voice of a Yegor.

APPROACHING LITERACY THROUGH STORIES

The purpose of this book is to address the growing need to help students, especially those new to English, achieve a higher level of literacy. This book offers teachers a meaningful approach to literacy instruction through folktales and personal stories. Giving learners the opportunity to tell, hear, write, read, and think about their own and others' tales provides them literacy experiences that can lead to achieving "critical literacy".[2] This form of literacy reaches beyond the skill of "calling words" and repeating the author's meaning. Rather, it utilizes these basic skills in order to relate the author's meaning to the reader's life experiences. Critical literacy grows in classrooms where basic language skills enable the exchange of meaningful expression. Teachers know that learning grows out of personal experience. They know that wherever you can connect the new to what students already know or need to know, powerful learning takes place. In recent years, this connection has become difficult to accomplish, in large part because of prescriptive instruction aimed at meeting requirements established far from local districts and their classroom settings.

In the broadest sense, the purpose of this book is to support teachers in their daily efforts to guide all students toward English literacy. By "all students," I mean the cross section of children who grace our classrooms, children who differ widely in race, class, religion, and, increasingly, in culture and language. Traditionally, this rich diversity inspired creative teaching even as it challenged teachers' work. I believe that recent programs intended to improve literacy achievement have burdened teachers with additional challenges that severely limit opportunities for creative teaching. The resulting curricular "diet" yields meager fare targeted at raising standardized test scores. Along with many others, I have come to believe that the No Child Left Behind Act, however well-intentioned, overburdens our schools with federal requirements that drain school budgets, limit instructional choices, and place undue focus on standardized test results.[3]

I believe that diversity provides learning opportunities for all students. We can enrich the path to English literacy by making full use of two of our greatest resources: diverse school populations and creative teaching.

NOTES

1. See Aarne, A. and Thompson, S. 1973 for a detailed folk tale classification system. Alan Dundes' *Cinderella: A Casebook* gives a thorough look at the Cinderella motif.

2. The following sources provide more on Critical Literacy: Bullock, A. 1975, Freire, P.1987; Giroux, H.1981; Harste, J., et al 1984; Smith, F. 1990.

3. Among the many critiques of the No Child Left Behind Act are: Meier, D. & Wood, G. (eds). 2004; Au, Wayne, 2004; Berlak, H. 2003; Taylor, D. 1998. Also, see the following Web sites: http://www.teacherleaders.org/resources/nclbres.htm1; http://www.fairtest.org/nattest/bushtest.html

PART ONE

The Power of *Story*

1

CHAPTER ONE

Immigrant Students
in Regular Classrooms

With the enjoyment of folk tales, children can assimilate a sense of their own cultural identity and an appreciation of others', and can share in the cultural literacy that should be the heritage of every child.

(Sutherland and Arbuthnot, 1991)

To read the word is to read the world.

(Freire, P. & Macedo, D., 1987)

This book aims to tap the power of stories—of telling, hearing, and writing favorite tales—and their potential for developing English literacy with both immigrant and nonimmigrant students in the regular classroom.

Schools in the United States serve increasing numbers of immigrant students whose first language is not English. This is not only true at the coasts, but also throughout the country. For example, in landlocked Kansas City, the number of non-English speaking students has exploded. Interviews with local educators appeared in a recent *Kansas City Star* article illustrating the extent of these increases (Adler, 04). One English Language Learners (ELL) coordinator explained:

> Just to tell you how we've grown, we have 20 elementary schools in our district. Three years ago there were four elementary schools that had ELL classes. Now, we have nine. Three years ago we had one high school that was an ELL site. Now it's all three. We have five middle schools. I have ELL in two. And I really need to open up a third site. We have logged more than 70 languages spoken in our schools. Our four top languages are Vietnamese, Arabic, Spanish and Bosnian. . . . We have Mende. We have lots of children speaking Ponapean from the Federated States of Micronesia. We have, of course, Farsi from Iran. We have French Creole. We have Urdu. Right now I have to find a Russian translator. We have Hakanese, Kurdish, Kswahill from Kenya. We have

Chinese, Cantonese Chinese. We have German. This is just
one elementary school" (Rica, S., 2004 emphasis in text).

These students spend the bulk of their school experience in the
regular classroom. By the regular classroom, I mean a classroom in a
public, private, or parochial school with students who generally are of
one age group and whose curriculum is designed to reach typical
students in that category. While there are variations (for example, family
groupings with a class made up of six-, seven-, and eight-year-olds), a
regular classroom configuration is most common throughout the United
States. In addition to typical students, these classrooms can include
students mainstreamed from specialized programs for those with
physical, mental, and/or behavior issues. Here we also find partial and
non-English speaking immigrant students.

As a teacher educator, I became aware of the need to prepare regular
classroom teachers for increasing numbers of immigrant students. When
English as a Second Language (ESL) teachers work closely with regular
classroom teachers, good things tend to happen. Unfortunately, not all
school districts have ESL programs, and in those that do, the amount and
quality of contact with regular classroom teachers can vary widely. For
example, an elementary teacher in a suburban school district in the
Midwest reported, "We have ESL only in the high school now, but hope
to add it to elementary school next year. I noticed that my ESL student
was modeling her mother's broken English. The high school ESL teacher
says she will try to come to help me, but I haven't seen her" (telephone
conversation May, 2001).

My first encounter with this need came when visiting one of my
student teachers. I asked about the boy sitting all by himself who seemed
to be doing nothing. "Oh," she replied, "That's Julio. He's from Mexico
and doesn't speak English. My cooperating teacher is waiting for him to
be tested for Special Ed." The next time I visited her, I brought along
another one of my students—a Spanish Education major. After she spoke
at length with Julio, she reported that he said he was especially good at
math, but was bored with most of the class work, all of which he had
studied in Mexico. He thought no one in his class even knew where
Mexico was. He said he felt weird and lonely. Sadly, the teacher did not
know of his math ability or how he felt. This case reminds us that
teachers "must resist the tendency to equate the use of a language other
than standard English with incompetence or lack of intelligence"
(Strickland and Alvermann, 2004).

What can be done to address this problem? We cannot expect
classroom teachers to speak the first language of all their students—nor
would being able to do so necessarily help students' transition to the
English language. "In our research," say Franquiz and de la Luz Reyes
"we have found that the use of students' own languages and, thus, their

own cultural knowledge as resources for learning, can be more important than a teacher's use of the students' languages" (1998).

It is also true that one does not need to be able to speak a student's first language to connect—to show sincere interest and respect. Yet, there is a need for some preparation of classroom teachers. Until recently, few states specified course requirements for certification that prepare prospective teachers to meet the needs of ESL students.[1]

When I thought of Julio's loneliness and detachment from learning, I began to wonder how to bridge this chasm. Something he said stayed with me, "No one in my class even knows where Mexico is." How sad that the English speakers in this class were not aware of Mexico and its rich culture. If they knew so little about our neighbor to the South, how much, I wondered, could they know or care to know about cultures from more distant lands such as Yegor's Azerbaijan? My wonderings led me to this study and to this book.

Over the course of one school year, I talked with immigrant students in three Midwestern school districts—one inner city, one suburban middle class, and one suburban upper-middle class. The students varied in age from seven to seventeen; from first to twelfth grade. They had been in the United States from one to three years. I visited each at least four times during the year collecting their stories and listening to them speak of their school experience. In between my visits, we wrote to each other via US mail. The students who participated in the study immigrated from Azerbaijan, Bosnia, Colombia, India, Iran, Korea, Laos, Mexico, and Somalia.

Currently, the United States is experiencing the greatest level of immigration since the 1920s with over ninety percent of recent immigrants coming from non-English-speaking countries. In the 1990s, when the US population grew by thirty-three million, about one-third were immigrants.

We need to acknowledge the influx of schoolchildren whose first language does not match that of the school, who are new to the culture, who often stumble as they try to fit into their new communities, and who, as a consequence, frequently drop out of school. According to the National Center for Education Statistics, there has been a steady increase over the past decade of more than twenty-six percent in the number of school-aged children who speak a language other than English at home and who speak English with difficulty. In the year 2000 census, the largest group represented was from Mexico, boosting the Hispanic count to record levels, according to the US Bureau of the Census and Population Reference Bureau. In March of 2005, the Office of English Language Acquisition reported that, "Based on the most currently available data from the states, there are approximately 5.1 million LEP students nationwide."

An array of acronyms refer to these students—LEP (Limited English Proficient), ESOL (English Speakers of Other Languages), ESL (English as a Second Language), and ELL (English Language Learners), to name a few. Throughout the book, I choose to use ELL (English Language Learners) because it projects a more positive image, and because it includes native English speakers.

Typically, after a brief stay in an ELL immersion area, limited English speaking students move to a regular classroom where they are mainstreamed with other students for most of the day. After that, the ELL teacher meets with them for short sessions until their English stabilizes. The regular classroom time can become a struggle for these students and their teachers. All too frequently, they feel that school is not a place where they feel accepted, where they see respect for their first culture, or where they know success in learning.

Unfortunately, the result is a high dropout rate among immigrant students. Low skill levels leave them with few options in a society remote from their experience. For many immigrant students, this represents a lost opportunity not only for their personal lives, but also for the students to fulfill a potentially meaningful contribution to their new country.

Assuring that immigrant students acquire English literacy remains a complex task, and our schools have a less than exemplary record in this regard. McLaughlin (1994) cites a study by the Council of Chief State School Officers indicating that "many language minority students do not receive the services they need in the educational system, are more likely to be held back, tracked in low academic groupings, or even placed in special education classes, and their dropout rates are alarmingly high."

The dropout problem is particularly true of Hispanic students, the largest immigrant group. A 1994 US General Accounting Office report[2] showed a forty-three percent dropout rate for Hispanic students not born in the United States. For all Hispanics, those born in the United States as well as those not, the National Center for Educational Statistics indicated that in 1999, twenty-nine percent of the dropouts were Hispanic compared to seven percent for whites and thirteen percent for blacks (2001).

Jacob and Jordan (1987) suggest two possible reasons for these dropouts: cultural differences between home and school and broader issues that work against good school performance. The broader issues include political, economic, and social forces that tend to establish prejudicial views of immigrants as subordinate to the mainstream culture. Addressing these broader issues goes beyond our purpose here. This book proposes a curriculum that can contribute toward positive home and school relationships.

Students new to our culture are typically impatient to feel "like real Americans". Schools (and sometimes the newcomers themselves) are too quick to shed their first culture ways. Sharing her extensive teaching experience, Christina Igoa points out that immigrant students need to maintain a sense of pride in their first culture and language as they integrate both worlds.[3] She cautions that "[t]he child who responds to unconscious mono-cultural attitudes is in danger of over-identifying with the new culture and sabotaging his or her own important roots" (1995). In maintaining contact with her students she has learned that most come to regret an early estrangement from their first culture and language.

As Ronald Takaki says, "The telling of stories liberates . . . telling and retelling of stories create communities of memory" (1999). It is my hope that sharing stories collected from students from so many different cultures and geographic areas, combined with stories shared by native English speaking students, will help to create "communities of memory" and mutual respect.

ORALITY AND LITERACY

Folktales begin with the spoken word. The oral tradition, with its informality and immediacy, provides direct and meaningful communication. Is this a kind of literacy? While some feel there are clear differences between orality and literacy, others see strong similarities

Walter Ong (1985) describes distinctions between oral and written expression. While some critics label his thoughts as simplistic, they can serve to clarify.[4]

Oral Thought	Written Thought
Situational	Abstract
Multi-directional	Linear
Immediate	Historical
Sound	Sight
Uses no tools	Uses pen/computer
Leaves no record	Leaves a record
A process	A product

More to our point here, we have learned that the opportunity to develop oral language advances the development of writing and reading.[5] Since folktales reflect deeply felt cultural beliefs shaped and reshaped to fit local contexts, they also hold potential as a powerful way to establish cross-cultural understanding. In effect, one could consider this another kind of literacy.

Becoming familiar with folktales provides children the opportunity to assimilate a sense of their own cultural identity while developing an appreciation for the culture of others. They can share in the cultural literacy that should be the heritage of every child. It is this awareness of other cultures, along with a spoken and print English literacy in an integrated curriculum, that forms the focus of this book.

Literacy: Oral or Textual

What opportunities exist in the regular classroom for ELL students to tap their rich personal histories in a risk-free setting, to hear positive models of English, and to relate what they hear and read to their life experience?

Unfortunately, supportive classroom environments for ELL students are not as common as one might hope. Troubling difficulties arise in our schools from assumptions about those not fluent in the English language. As we saw with Julio, this can result in misidentification—of not knowing much, or, worse, having little capacity to learn or to become literate.

But, what exactly is literacy? Must it only take a written, textual form, or can oral expression count as a kind of literacy? Attempting to determine whether a culture is literate or non-literate can become problematical resulting in false assumptions about both literate and oral cultures. Some feel that no "either/or" labels are appropriate because literacy grows and changes over time and is determined by those directly experiencing it.[6] Fernandez suggests a multifaceted concept of literacy that avoids the shortcomings of "either/or" labels (2001). From her perspective, the concept of literacy grows and changes over time, determined by those directly experiencing it.

The instructional strategies suggested in this book were selected to provide both oral and written language stepping-stones to English literacy.

English Language Literacy

The literacy level of the general population in the United States is a major national concern. Business and industry complain that a high school diploma does not guarantee the ability to read directions or to write reports or memos. Big companies, such as Sprint have found the need to provide remedial reading programs for employees (2000).

In spite of the fact that the United States compulsory education requires school attendance until the age of 16, ten years of schooling does not seem to be enough for the general population. This raises questions about the effectiveness of literacy instruction—an important factor contributing to gaps in literacy achievement (Alvermann 2004). In what follows, I attempt to clarify my view of teaching English literacy in school.

The best way to approach literacy instruction in schools remains a continuing issue of controversy. It is remarkable that over one hundred years ago, educators argued this issue[7] as they do today. Over the years, there have been recurrent pressures to emphasize a molecular, direct phonics approach to teaching literacy that recede temporarily only to reappear and recede again. These pressures have influenced second language teaching as well.[8]

Many US schools identify decoding and reading comprehension as end goals for reading instruction[9]. However, this view bypasses a crucial component of literacy—that of *considering what the author says*. In other words, it is not enough to merely repeat the author's message, but rather, to build upon the comprehension stage and tap what the reader thinks about the author's message. Because this conception of literacy, often referred to as "critical literacy," entails connecting what is read to the reader's life, it has a political quality, which, while present in any consideration of literacy acquisition, becomes more evident in this form. Some feel that this political quality represents one possible reason for the repeated shifts back to a bit-by-bit, phonics emphasis for literacy instruction.[10] Many believe, and I agree, that this political quality energizes the process of becoming literate and gives the learner a sense of agency in his world.[11] I believe that in a country founded on the notion of a participatory democracy, critical literacy represents a basic need.

Another useful conception of literacy acquisition consistent with this perspective is the "transactional" view—a view that assumes a transaction between the reader and the text in which the reader establishes or constructs meaning.[12] Also known as a "constructivist" model, it grew out of a number of sources including philosophy and linguistics (Applebee, 1991). Based on the influential work of pioneers in the field of language and learning, this perspective not only sees the learner actively engaged in creating meaning, but also influenced by the environment in its construction. A transactional approach to literacy acquisition takes into account the process of learning as well as what is learned. For example, it acknowledges the positive impact of utilizing heterogeneous groupings of students where interaction among students of various background and ability levels encourages varied responses—a major change from traditional approaches, which tend to group students by similarity.

Orality: The Call of Stories

The connection between personal knowledge and school knowledge represents a major link in language learning and in learning generally.[13] This book utilizes this connection by emphasizing students' folktales, family tales, and stories of their experiences. The curriculum invites immigrant students to share tales they remember from their first culture—tales told to them by family members, teachers, or others in the community. It encourages native English-speaking students to do the same.

The tales collected from the immigrant students represented here were recorded and then transcribed exactly as they were told—warts and all—in order to maintain their personal quality and to preserve the charm of their own voices. (Correct English versions of each story are in copy-ready form in the Appendix.)

The ELL students shared their stories by writing and telling them in their first languages as well as in English. This was not only to help them feel a sense of cultural pride, but also to avoid the sense of estrangement often experienced when ties to a first culture are absent or abandoned in new surroundings. The Native English speakers also benefit, not only by sharing their own stories, but from seeing and hearing other languages, thus expanding cultural knowledge and understanding. Moreover, this exposure serves as a vehicle for all students to interact. In their explorations of classroom relationships of native English speakers and ELL students, Valdes (2001) and Norton (2000) learned that native English speakers typically avoid meaningful exchanges with English language learners. They tend to see ELL students as strange, rather than admiring them for knowing more than one language.

Telling stories in their first languages helps ELL students connect personal knowledge and school knowledge, a powerful link to learning. As with any task asked of them, ELL students need what Krashen calls "comprehensible input" (1982). That is, teachers need to take care to assure that ELL students understand the focus of the task by utilizing a variety of forms of explanation. At the same time, competent English-speakers in the class benefit from teachers' clearly presented expectations.

Oral or Print Literacy

Today's world tends to favor print literacy over the spoken word. This is in spite of theories that link oral thought to the development of human consciousness.[14] A print literacy bias has not always been universal. Scribner & Cole found that not only does the lack of ability to write language have no particular impact upon cognitive ability, it is not even considered a particularly important skill among the Vai people of Liberia (1970).

Walter Ong acknowledges the crucial role of oral language as well as the positive characteristics of written thought.[15] He believes that orality is more natural than print literacy since it does not have to be formally "acquired". The ever accelerating move toward electronic communication and the proliferation of media have even led some to favor orality with the view that print literacy is dead or dying (McLuhan & Fiore, 1967).

I believe educators need to provide their students both oral and textual language opportunities for literacy acquisition. Rather than emphasize the distinctions between orality and literacy, I suggest we explore ways they might complement each other. For example, students could retell, orally or in writing, folk tales, family histories, and memorable personal stories, as the strategies found in the following chapters suggest.

The rationale for having children retell their stories orally as well as in written form comes from the view that oral language differs from written language. While structurally related, one does not really represent the other. In other words, writing is not 'talk written down'. Moreover, we have learned that the process of integrating all the forms of discourse—speaking, listening, reading, writing, and thinking—reinforces each of them. [16]

Story: A Narrative Approach to Literacy

Asking immigrant students to retell meaningful stories has great potential. A number of influential educators have recognized the impact of narrative on learning. For example, Bruner (1986) identifies narrative as one of two basic models or "ways of ordering experience" and the other, a logical, sequential approach. Harold Rosen feels schools should increase time devoted to narrative experiences because they almost exclusively deliver time and curriculum in Bruner's logical format. Rosen suggests approaches such as Retelling, an oral or written narrative instructional strategy that, "[g]iven the liberating encouragement of the teacher, . . . can be a profoundly creative activity" (1988). Because the Retelling strategy does not entail memorization (that is, reproducing the original text, per se), it frees students to create narratives in ways characteristic of the oral tradition. Betty Rosen, who used retellings with great success in teaching English to disaffected London students, found the language abilities revealed in their retellings surprisingly impressive.[17]

The universal "call of stories" has had a long and continuing attraction. Many believe that folklore meets deep-seated sociological, psychological, and developmental needs.[18] The fact that the stories grow out of the oral tradition—that they are told and retold, changing slightly with each version and each cultural perspective and, yet, maintaining the same motifs—tells us that they endure because they are enduringly meaningful.

A narrative curriculum has a strong impact on all learners. As Lauritzen and Jaeger indicate, "Not only are stories long remembered, but the learning that is generated from story and intertwined with story is long remembered" (1998).

POSSIBILITIES FOR POSITIVE LEARNING

Tied to the need to prepare immigrant students for productive lives is the general need to prepare all students to live in a pluralistic society. Sleeter indicates that demographic changes in the United States "increase the likelihood that any American child today will grow up working and possibly living with other Americans who differ culturally, linguistically, and/or racially" (1994). Au reported that her school experience sharing stories and family memories with immigrant children "brought the class together as a community. [They] sensed they had experiences similar to those of their classmates" (1993).

BEFORE WE BEGIN

Before we look at the stories shared by immigrant students and explore ways to utilize them in classrooms, consider the following two options. One is a memoir of a student who found herself in a situation where school was a world of strangeness that surrounded and isolated her. The other is an activity designed to help identify and rethink the way perceptions of the world can impact our expectations and our attitudes about others.

Sharing these with your students could help establish a meaningful connection to the lessons that follow, for both immigrant and nonimmigrant students.

A MEMOIR

The following selection comes from *Harmony in a World of Difference,* a multicultural curriculum (1986, Anti-defamation League of B'nai B'rith). Perhaps it can help personalize the issues facing immigrant students. Written by a student, Noy Chou, it speaks for itself.

You Have to Live in Somebody Else's Country to Understand

By Noy Chou

What is it like to be an outsider?

What is it like to sit in the class where everyone has blond hair and you have black hair?

What is it like when the teacher says, "Whoever wasn't born here raise your hand."

And you are the only one.

Then, when you raise your hand, everybody looks at you and makes fun of you.

You have to live in somebody else's country to understand.

What is it like when the teacher treats you like you've been here all your life?

What is it like when the teacher speaks too fast and you are the only one who can't understand what he or she is saying and you try to tell him or her to slow down.

Then when you do, everybody says, "If you don't understand, go to a lower class or get lost."

You have to live in somebody else's country to understand.

What is it like when you are an opposite?

When you wear the clothes of your country and they think you are crazy to wear these clothes and you think they are pretty.

You have to live in somebody else's country to understand.

What is it like when you are always a loser?

What is it like when somebody bothers you when you do nothing to them?

You tell them to stop but they tell you that they didn't do anything to you.

Then, when they keep doing it until you can't stand it any longer, you go up to the teacher and tell him or her to tell them to stop bothering you.

They say that they didn't do anything to bother you.

He says, "Yes, she didn't do anything to her" and you have no witness to turn to.

So, the teacher thinks you are a liar.

You have to live in somebody else's country to understand.

What is it like when you try to talk and you don't pronounce the words right?

They don't understand you.

They laugh at you but you don't know that they are laughing at you, and you start to laugh with them. They say, "Are you crazy, laughing at yourself? Go get lost, girl."

You have to live in somebody else's country without a language to understand.

What is it like when you walk in the street and everybody turns around to look at you and you don't know that they are looking at you.

Then, when you find out, you want to hide your face but you don't know where to hide because they are everywhere.

You have to live in somebody else's country to feel it.

A fifth-grade teacher reports her experience using this piece with her class:

> This was a very powerful reading. I began by reading it to the children. We held a class discussion about how the Statue of Liberty relates to this story. Why is she there? Do we live up to her promises? I then had them read it to themselves. After reading it, they had fun with "written conversation" which is still one of my favorite activities. [For an explanation of the Written Conversation Strategy, see page 63.] Here is a short excerpt from one journal:

Student #1: At church on Sunday, . . . I saw a lady in a long robe. It was really pretty. I think she was from another country. She had a dot on her head. Did you see her?

Student #2: No, I didn't.

Student #1: I took her downstairs and helped her get a doughnut.

Student #2: That was really nice. I've never been to another country.

Student #1: Neither have I. I think it would be hard.

This fifth grade teacher, who teaches in a parochial school, continues:

> We were in the middle of a unit on missionary saints. We held a class discussion about how some saints 'lived in somebody else's country' and what that must have been like. We talked about facing different languages, customs, and religions. The students then wrote reflections about this. Here's one example:
>
> *I think that St. Francis X sometimes felt bad kind of because he was in a strange land. I know I would. I wonder if he couldn't understand some of those places' languages. I wonder if he was the only one with white skin or something like that in school. I wonder if no one liked him.*

AN ACTIVITY

Here is an activity that reveals students' perceptions of the world—the continents and their comparative size. Most of us are familiar with the Mercator projection map of the world developed in Germany in 1569. The Mercator projection, which places Europe and Germany in the center of the map, distorts the size of the continents, especially areas south of the equator. Europe appears larger than it really is and Greenland looks bigger than Africa. In the Peters projection developed in 1974, landmass shapes and sizes differ dramatically from the more commonly used

Mercator projection (Gutstein, 2001).[19] As a result, our image of the continents can be somewhat unrealistic. Once identified, the resulting misconceptions can bring a more realistic view of the world.

Valuable insights can emerge when students consider the impact this might have on perceptions of the relative importance of countries/ cultures. It could help move away from an overly Americanized, Euro-centric dominated world-view.

Harlan Rimmerman (2000) presented this activity to graduate students with powerful results. He has also presented it successfully at the elementary and secondary levels. It proved to be a highly effective strategy that exposed students' images of how the world is arranged, and how our perceptions can impact our values.

The activity challenges small groups of students to tear paper into the size and shape of the continents and then arrange the shapes into a map. Each group is given one 36 x 36 inch piece of brown butcher paper, four 8 1/2 x 11 inch sheets of paper, and a glue stick. Their maps are shared and compared with official maps—both Mercator and Peters projections. Discussion can lead to seeing how distortions can change our view of the relative importance of country, culture, and race.

NOTES

1. See Garcia, G.E., Willis, A.I., & Harris, V.J., 1988 for more about teacher certification requirements.

2. The 1994 US General Accounting Office report, Hispanics' Schooling, Risk factors for Dropping out and Barriers to Resume Education. Also, the 2001 National Center for Educational Statistics Report.

3. With *The Inner World of the Immigrant Child* (1995), Igoa shares an in depth look at her immigrant students. Igoa expresses concern about the many pressures to replace rather than supplement native language and culture.

4. See George, R. 1985 *Orality & Literacy* for a critique of Ong.

5. Sadly, the value of "Talk" as an important skill equal to reading and writing has little place in most US classrooms. Reduced to a disciplinary measure, talk becomes something to avoid. Among those who remind us of its usefulness are: Smith, F, Moffett, J., Holdaway, D, and Halliday, M.A.K. .

6. Fernandez 2001 provides more on a multifaceted conception of literacy.

7. For a history of the on-going controversy see: Mathews, M. 1966; Smith, N.B. 1965. For contemporary arguments see: Shannon & Goodman 1994, Routman 1996, Pearson 1997, Taylor, D. 1999, Fernandez, R. 2001, Strickland, D. & Alvermann, D. 2004, Gregory, G. & Ksuzmich, L. 2005.

8. See Gandara, P. 1994, Freeman, 1988, and Krashen, S.K. 1981.

9. A sampling of the numerous writers addressing this issue: Goodman, K., et al. 1988; Shannin, 1994; Garan, E. 2002; Krashen, S.K. 2002.

10. See: Goodman, K., et al, 1988, Shannon & Goodman, 1994, Routman, R., 1996, Creighton, D. 1997, and Taylor, D. 1998.

11. These thinkers are among those who feel the whole purpose of becoming literate is to provide a sense of agency: Giroux, H. 1981, McLaren, P. 1989, Freire, P. 1970, 1987.

12. See Rosenblatt, L. 1978, Harste, et al, 1984.

13. Among them are: Vygotsky 1986, Halliday, 1975, Giroux, 1981, Freire, P. 1987

14. See Jaynes, J. 1976 and Ong, W. 1988.

15. See: Ong, W. 1978, 1983. 1986

16. See: Smith, F. 1984, 1990, Altwerger, et al 1987, Moffett, J. 1992.

17. Betty Rosen's *And None of it was Nonsense,* 1988 provides an inspiring account of the retellings of her disaffected London students.

18. Fields related to Education have utilized narrative effectively. For example, in the field of Psychiatry, Robert Coles' *The Call of Stories* 1989 narrative yielded powerful results, as it did in his earlier interviews of children, the *Children of Crisis* series. Hero stories abound in the field of Anthropology as in *Masks of God* series by Joseph Campbell 1964, 1966, 1968. Bettleheim 1976 suggested that fairy tales address real psychological issues in childhood. Zipes, J. 1983 presented fairy tales as a tool for socialization in his *The Trials and Tribulations of Little Red Riding Hood.*

19. Eric Gutstien (2001) explains how the Mercator projection distorts. For example, Greenland appears about the same size as Africa, but Africa is actually 14 times larger.

PART TWO

A Gathering of Tales

Part Two contains stories gathered directly from the immigrant students. Chapter Two, *One Story and Its Travels*, addresses the universality of folktales and their potential for bridging cultural differences, along with practical suggestions for their use. To illustrate this, I look at three versions of the same story shared by students from three vastly different cultures.

SUGGESTED INSTRUCTIONAL STRATEGIES

To support literacy, each chapter provides suggested instructional strategies to help incorporate these tales into the reading, language arts, or English curriculum. Research by Marzano, Pickering, et al (2001) shows that when instructional strategies are compatible with what we know about brain function and the learning process, higher student performance results.

The strategies suggested in this book meet these criteria. Designed to be carried out in a nonthreatening environment, they support social interaction, and encourage free expression of ideas in an oral, written, kinesthetic, or visual format. The following chart takes a sample of these instructional strategies and rates them in relation to performance gain, brain research, and literacy tactics.

Teacher discretion based on age level and students' knowledge should determine which age groups would be most appropriate for the strategies found throughout this book. Teachers know all too well that student age groups are full of surprises. An activity presumed to be appropriate for younger students sometimes works successfully with those who are older and vice versa. With that said, I recommend these strategies for upper elementary or middle school students.

Impact of Instructional Strategies

Strategy	Percent Performance Gain	Brain Research	Literacy Tactics
Mandalas (Analogies/Metaphors)	45%	Brain seeks patterns, connections.	Compare/contrast, classifying, concept formation, etc.
Venn Diagrams (Generating nonlinguistic representations)	28%	Visual stimuli recalled with 90% accuracy	Graphic Organizers
Cubing (Cooperative learning, collaboration)	27%	Brain is social, seeks interaction/ dialogue	Small group projects

(Adapted from Gregory & Kuzmich 2005, p 11)

BASIC CHARACTERISTICS OF FOLKTALES

Students will need some basic background information about folktales to benefit fully from these strategy suggestions. The Appendix contains a listing of additional useful folktale resources.

The following basic characteristics should help expand students' knowledge and give them a genre focus.

Introductions and Conclusions: Both the introduction and conclusion of folktales are characteristically brief. In a sentence or two the scene is set; the action starts. The conclusion typically ties together all details presented in the introduction in one or two sentences.

Characterization: Character development stays at a surface level. Typically, folks that populate these stories are either all good or all bad.

Story Development: Folktales usually present a limited number of simple, straightforward incidents. For example, one recurring story pattern follows a sequence of "threes"—three brothers, three pigs, three bears. Plots generally take a direct, noncomplex route.

Style: A simple and precise style is typical. Short sentences dominate with little attention to description. This genre utilizes repetition, predictable patterns of speech and conversational tone.

Theme: While not always formally stated, a simple reason usually permeates the story, for example, good conquers evil, kindness overrides meanness, hard work is rewarded.

SPECIAL CONSIDERATIONS FOR ELL STUDENTS

Some guidelines are in order for regular classroom teachers who have had little or no experience working with ELL students. While clarification of expectations, directions for tasks, and general content are necessary for all students, it is crucial for students new to English. The concept of "comprehensible input" (Krashen, 1982) is a good rule of thumb. Wherever possible, topics and the tasks that grow out of class discussions need to be clearly understood. It's better to err on the side of too much explanation, rather than to assume that what works with native English speakers will do. Consider increasing the use of nonverbal forms of communication to reinforce verbal directions. A graphic organizer, a simple picture, or a gesture will help clarify as you speak. Marzano, Pickering, et al. found that using "nonlinguistic representation" increased performance gain for students by twenty-eight percent (2001). The success of the suggestions and strategies in the following chapters will depend upon students' understanding of the topic and the task.

TEN STRATEGIES FOR MONOLINGUAL TEACHERS OF BILINGUAL STUDENTS

1. Arrange for bilingual aides or parent volunteers to read literature written in the primary language of the students and then to discuss what they have read. Plan for older students who speak the first language of the children to come to the class regularly to read to or, with younger students, to act as cross-age tutors.
2. Set up a system of pen-pal letters written in the primary language between students of different classes or different schools.
3. Have students who are bilingual pair up with classmates who share the same primary language but are more proficient in English. This buddy system is particularly helpful for introducing new students to class routines.
4. Invite bilingual storytellers to come to the class and tell stories that would be familiar to all the students. Using context clues, these storytellers can convey familiar stories in languages other than English. Well-known stories such as Cinderella have counter parts (and origins) in non-English languages.
5. Build a classroom library of books in languages other than English. This is essential for primary language literacy development. At times, teachers within a school may want to pool these resources.
6. To increase the primary language resources in classrooms, publish books in languages other than English. Allow bilingual students to share their stories with classmates.

7. Encourage journal writing in the first language. A bilingual aide or parent volunteer can read and respond to journal entries. Give students a choice of language in which to read and write.

8. Look around the room at the environmental print. Include signs in the first language as well as articles and stories in English about the countries the students come from.

9. Use videotapes produced professionally or by students to support learning and raise self-esteem.

10. Have students engage in oral activities, such as show and tell using their first language as they explain objects, games, or customs from their homelands.

(S.E. Freeman & Y. S. Freeman, 1992; Y. S. Freeman & D. E. Freeman, 1991 as quoted in Weaver, C., 1999)

TEN MORE STRATEGIES TO HELP FACILITATE UNDERSTANDING IN CLASSROOMS WITH ENGLISH LANGUAGE LEARNERS

1. Read written directions aloud and write oral directions on the board.

2. If you don't understand a student's English, repeat what the student has said with question intonation.

3. Rather than identify errors in language, simply restate them correctly.

4. Periodically give students short vocabulary lists—either English to Native Language or English to simpler English.

5. Simplify hard words before lesson or activity by providing the student a glossary of difficult words.

6. When you see that a child is having trouble understanding what others have said or asked, simplify as much as possible. For example, if someone asks, "How does our government blatantly and maliciously infringe on our freedom?" rephrase as "How does our government infringe on our freedom?"

7. Since English is so idiomatic, teach an idiom whenever possible.

8. Have students, as part of an on-going assignment, create and maintain their own picture dictionary. They can be kept in both their native language and in English.

9. During communication, use as many different forms of body language as possible.

10. Set time for peer tutoring about once a week. This is good for those students who need help and it acts as a self-esteem builder for those who give help.

(Compiled by Verdesco, J., 2000. Taken from: Callahan, Clark & Kellough, 1995; Friend & Bursuck, 1996; and conversations with Delhalle-Ritzka, F. & Comstock, J., 1997.)

CHAPTER TWO

One Story and Its Travels

The old tales inspire not only the obvious reactions of laughter or tears, but also the deeper sense of a story linking us to human lives over the ages, a story that has been told time and time again in many parts of the world.

(Sutherland & Arbuthnot.1991)

The three stories presented below illustrate how a common story motif can appear in vastly different cultures. Although these three children had never met each other, each shared this story after the simple prompt, "Tell me a story that you remember." They were recent immigrants to the United States who attended three different schools in three different school districts. Their countries of origin are Bosnia, Iran, and Korea. Yet, each tale is basically the same story type (Aarne & Thompson, 1973).

Why do such similar stories appear in such diverse cultures?

This question continues to puzzle and fascinate. Some say all folk stories come from one major source. Sometimes referred to as the *monogenesis* theory (Sutherland, 1991), it argues that the tales all came out of a Germanic/ Scandinavian source. According to this view, they were distributed by land and by sea as explorers and merchants traveling trade routes expanded knowledge of the Western world.

Others make a strong argument for a many-source view. They say that all humans share a need to explain their world, to vilify evil and reward good, to give meaning to their lives through *story*. This perspective is sometimes known as the *polygenesis* theory (Sutherland, 1991). It refers to a deeply rooted psychological need that establishes the essence of our humanity.

Both views acknowledge the strong pull of these stories—whether they were first told by travelers/voyagers to far off lands, or whether they emanated from deep within a "collective sub-consciousness" (Jung, 1964). Perhaps this explains how we have come to find so many versions of the same story throughout the world.

How can we use this similarity of a story line to bridge the cultural gap that increases as our immigrant population increases? I attempt to address this question in a practical sense through an integrated curriculum approach that follows various articulations of common story motifs.

The following three versions of the same tale provide a starting point for classroom discussion of alternative versions of the same tale found in vastly different cultures.

This tale is familiar to most Euro-Western peoples as the story of "The Wolf and the Seven Little Kids" from the Brothers Grimm. (A copy-ready form of this version of the tale can be found in the Appendix for classroom use.)

First, you will find the tales themselves followed by some possible instructional strategies for classroom follow up.

Please note: Feel free to copy any of these student's tales for classroom use. They are available in copy-ready form in the Appendix. As was stated previously, all tales were transcribed verbatim—just as students told them—in order to provides a true example of the oral tradition in its raw, first-told (first draft) form. The grammatical errors, so typical of new English speakers, remain. This not only preserves the simplicity of the folktale genre, it provides a true student *voice*. Here is one reader's response to this approach:

> I like the way the stories are told in students' own words; I can imagine that this would increase the odds of students being comfortable retelling stories that they know. When I do a storytelling unit, one obstacle students have to overcome is their temptation to memorize the story in the form they found it, rather than making it their own. These are so obviously "oral" stories written down that I believe the transition would be easier than from "written" stories derived from oral traditions.

However, others disagree. They feel that ELL students need correct models of English; that these students should avoid incorrect examples. Another reader responds:

> There were run-on's, errors in verb tense and/or form, and sentence structure errors based on word choice or omission. If literacy is a goal, not only orality but also written literacy, then, of course, the students must have an exemplary written modal, if not an authentic piece of literature, as in this case, at least an error-free student version.

Because each makes a valid point, I have included correct English versions of the tales in copy-ready form in the Appendix.

You can choose which you prefer to use.

The Five Little Goats, Their Mother, and the Big Bad Wolf

Told by Zulfo, a third-grade student from Bosnia.

Once upon a time there lived five little goats and their mother. They lived in a little house beside the river and on the other side of the river lived a big, bad wolf.

One sunny day mother and her five little ones ran out of food. The mother told the five little ones to not open the door to anybody 'til she comes back.

Later the wolf came across the river and knocked on the door. The five little goats answered, "Who is it?" And the wolf said, "It's mother." But the five little goats looked under the door and saw that his feet were brown, so it must have been the wolf.

So the wolf tried again. He colored his feet white and said, "It's mother. I'm home. Open up."

The mother goat came by and saw the wolf trying to get in, so the mother kicked the wolf into the river. The five little goats were safe.

And, for the wolf, he was all wet and soaked. He went home mad.

The little goats and their mother lived happily ever after.

Little Bunny and Two Little Sisters

Told by Rena, a third-grade student from Iran.

Once upon a time there was a little bunny who had two little sisters and one day their mother was going out to buy some bread. So, their mother said, "Be careful for the wolf!" "OK," they said.

So their mother went.

And then someone knocked on the door and the three little sisters said, "Who is it?" And the wolf showed his hand. It was gray, not white like their mother's hand. The little sisters said, "We will not open the door!" This happened five times. So the wolf went away.

Later the door knocked again and they said, "Who is it?" And the wolf showed his hand. This time it was white. He had covered it with flour. The little sisters opened the door. So, the wolf ate two of them. The other one hid.

So when the mom came back she saw only one of them that was saved. This one told the story that happened and they both went and tore open the wolf's stomach and the two bunnies got out and they all lived happily ever after.

The Brother, the Sister, and the Wolf

Told by Chul, a middle-school student from Korea.

Once there was a family with a brother and a sister. Every day the mother went to work to sell bread. She said to her children, "Don't open the door to anyone but me." And they said, "OK."

One day she went to work and when she was coming back, she met a wolf. Wolf told her if she gives him a piece of bread he'll not hurt her. She gives him a piece of bread. This happens three times. The third time she didn't have any bread so the wolf ate the mother.

The wolf dressed up like the mother and went to the children's house. He said that he was their mother, but the brother said, "You are not our mother. Your voice doesn't sound like her." The wolf went away. Next time he ate an egg to make his voice sound softer. When he got there they asked him to put his hand out and his arm to see if it was the mother's. They opened the door because the wolf had their mother's dress on with long sleeves.

When the wolf came in he said he was very tired and they should go to sleep. So they all laid down. The children then felt the wolf's arm and it was very hairy with scratchy hair, so they knew it wasn't their mother. They tried to run away. The wolf chased them. The children got into bed and prayed for a rope and a rope came down and they climbed up it to the sky. The wolf prayed for a rope, too. The wolf climbed up and when he got kind of high, the rope fell down and down came the wolf.

The brother became the sun and the sister became the moon. But, because the sister was afraid of the dark, they changed places and the sister became the sun and the brother became the moon.

CLASSROOM POSSIBILITES

What does it mean when students from three disparate parts of the world who attend different schools in three different school districts, and who, unknown and apart from one another, tell the same story with only minor variations? If nothing else, it provides an opportunity to show how *story* can link dissimilar cultures.

Consider the following suggestions as possible starting-off points. For teachers who have taught English Language Learners and who might be familiar with these or similar strategies, some new insights can be gained from the applications suggested here. For teachers with little or no such experience, these strategies can fill a very practical need.

Before students read and discuss the stories, consider a brief focus lesson, a warm-up to highlight the topic right before beginning a new area of study (Atwell, N., 1998). This approach does not aim to provide a comprehensive overview, but rather, to whet students' interest in a new topic or to remind them of what they might already know. The emphasis here is on "brief" and "right before" in order to give immediate focus to the lesson. To demonstrate that similar stories are told in dissimilar geographic areas/cultures, you could display a collection of Cinderella stories to be read to and/or by the class at a later time. (See the Appendix for a Cinderella bibliography) Sharing brief excerpts from examples such as *The Rough Face Girl* (Martin, R., Shannon, D., 1992) a Native American version; *Yeh Shen* (Ai-Ling, L, Young, E., 1982), a Chinese version; or *Cinderella* (Perrault, C., Brown, Marcia, 1954), the French version, demonstrates the vast geographic impact of this one tale. While these versions came from extremely different cultures, the story line—the *type* or *motif*—remained constant.

Encourage the class to look for and keep track of as many different versions of folktales they may find from different cultures/geographic areas. As they read or hear tales, help them focus on the similarities and differences between the stories, as well as the location of countries and cultures represented.

Once students have heard or read the three variants of the tale, *The Nanny Goat and Her Kids,* teacher and students could share other versions of this tale that they might know (see additional titles at the end of this chapter), then build upon this discussion with one of the following approaches. Or, better still, use one of the teacher's own design.

People, Plot, and Place Maps

The People, Plot, and Place Maps strategy is a variation of Time and Place Maps (Jacobson, J. 1998). It provides the opportunity for students to compare and contrast locations and cultures, as well as character, plot, and setting in a visual format. The idea here is to promote critical analysis of the stories and emphasize the universality of the tale type and to expand students' knowledge of the three cultures represented. This approach will probably work best with middle-school students.

Each work group researches one of the stories using a simple outline map of Iran, Korea, or Bosnia to identify and map out 1) geographic characteristics of the countries/cultures, and 2) the story characters, plot, and setting. Some knowledge of mapping and creating legends for maps would be useful. One source for a simple map and general information about each country can be found at http://www.odci.gov/cia/publications/factbook/geos/ks.html. Once the maps are completed, students reconvene to share their written and/or oral interpretations of their findings. They discuss similarities and differences and consider possible cultural influences that may have shaped these versions. For example, they could consider the impact of Bosnia being a landlocked country compared to Korea at the southern half of a peninsula with water on all but the north, or with Iran's location surrounded by the Caspian Sea, the Persian Gulf, and the Gulf of Omar. And yet, the story from Bosnia is the only one that mentions water. (The wolf lives on the other side of the river. The mother kicks the wolf into the river and he gets soaked) Korea is an Asian country, Bosnia is European, and Iran is Middle Eastern, each with a distinctive cultural heritage. Finally, they make a guess, supported by their findings, about how they think the story came to be present in three such distinct cultures.

Role, Audience, Form, and Theme

Another approach called Role, Audience, Form, and Theme (RAFT) and created by Dueck (1986) asks students to take on a specified role and have a specific audience in mind for a piece they will write. Here again, I recommend this strategy for students in middle school. The writer pretends to be a character who addresses another character or group. Students work in pairs as they write or talk through a piece from the perspective of a particular role directed at a particular audience. Speaking with the whole class, the teacher solicits a list of characters or persons either in the story or living at the time and place from which the story came. Another list solicits a possible audience for the written piece. The final list collects possible forms for their ideas to take. These might be transferred onto cards for distribution or simply listed in clusters. For example:

RAFT Strategy Example

Possible author	Possible audience	Possible form
a character in one story	another character in the story	Newspaper article
Big Bad Wolf in Zulfo's story	(Mother Goat in Zulfo's story)	
a character in one story	similar character in another story	Scene in a play
(Wolf in Chul's story)	(Wolf in Rena's story)	
storyteller from Iran	one of the students in the class	Science fiction

When the results are shared with the class, they are asked to critique the way the stories portray the author, audience, and format.

This strategy can function in a number of communication formats: oral language, with students acting out situations in role-play; visually, with students drawing or painting the interactions; movement, with students interpreting through dance; and of course, writing, with students' written compositions.

The following newspaper article was written by two sixth graders.

Wolf Denies Bad Deed

Kansas City. On Wednesday, March 3rd, Mr. Wolf was seen at the house of Mrs. Bunny and her three little bunnies. A neighbor, Mrs. Cat, said she saw Mr. Wolf pounding on the door.

"He went away and came back several times," said Mrs. Cat.

The police report says that Mr. Wolf says he was just paying a friendly visit. But the bunnies say he got into the house by pretending to be their mother. He ate two of the bunnies and then left. When Mrs. Bunny returned, she found the one bunny and cut the other two out of the wolf's tummy. Mr. Wolf said he didn't do it and blames Mrs. Bunny for his very bad tummy ache.

Sing-Along Song

Sing-Along Song is group singing in the style of "follow the bouncing ball." When groups watch the lyrics as they sing a simple tune, they acquire both pronunciation and meaning of new vocabulary words. Paul Markham of the University of Kansas says one of the biggest advantages of using group singing is that it lowers natural anxiety and inhibition when trying to speak another language. While he said it is true that singing lyrics can produce some distortions, such as the length of syllables and sentence structure, it also can improve pronunciation, and the tune helps with recall (2004). Charlene Littlefield, an ELL teacher, was so enthusiastic about her students' response to singing that she won a grant to purchase a karaoke machine for her classroom. She says the karaoke speakers help because "[t]hey hear their own voices amplified. It helps them self-correct their pronunciation" (2004). But a karaoke machine isn't necessary to take advantage of this strategy. Lyrics projected from a simple overhead projector works well. Or, simply have students follow lyrics printed on a chart or chalkboard. It's important to use your hand or a pointer to follow the words, thus guiding students' vision as they sing. All simple songs work well: *I've Been Working on the Railroad; The Bear Went Over the Mountain; London Bridge is Falling Down;* etc. An example for our purposes might use *Shoo Fly Don't Bother Me*

Shoo Fly don't bother me	Shoo Wolf don't bother us
Shoo fly don't bother me	Shoo Wolf don't bother us
Shoo fly don't bother me	Shoo Wolf don't bother us
For I belong to somebody	For we will surely make a fuss.
I feel, I feel, I feel,	You're not, you're not, you're not
I feel like a morning star	You're not our Mother dear
I feel, I feel, I feel	You're not, you're not, you're not
I feel like a morning star	And that is very clear!

To find more song ideas from cultures around the world, visit Momma Lisa's World at this web site: http:www.momalisa.com/world/mdex.html.

Sketch to Stretch

Here is a variation of Sketch to Stretch (Rhodes, 1989), which was developed by Seigel (1984). This strategy provides students who are in the process of acquiring stronger language skills an expanded vehicle to express their response to the stories through a visual format. It exposes them to a more complex example, which they can incorporate into their sketch, and it gives them the opportunity to develop oral language as they describe their sketches to the class. This should be appropriate for upper elementary-age students.

The class summarizes the stories told by Zulfo, Rena, and Chul after reading all three versions. The teacher then reads a more elaborate version of the same tale, for example, Grimm's version. Working in small groups or in pairs, the students make a sketch that would summarize all four stories—Grimm's and the three told by Chul, Rena, and Zulfo. Next, they share their sketches with the entire class pointing out the connections to the readings and explaining why they chose to illustrate them in the way they did. How would topography and weather in the three different locations influence students' illustrations? What might the scenery look like? How the characters might be dressed?

Comparing the three versions offers additional insights. Students can identify the similarities: the wolf is the common enemy who disguises himself; the mother is protective; children disobey; etc. They can point out differences: Rena and Zulfo's stories feature animals (bunnies and goats) while Chul's story centers around a human family. All the kids survive in Rena's and Boris' stories while in Chul's story the mother is eaten and not revived and the two kids rise into the sky. The appendix provides the brothers Grimm's *The Wolf and the Seven Kids* in copy-ready form. Distributing copies of this tale could provide a variety of learning experiences. For example, students could work in small groups to perform a script for a radio or TV dramatization. They could cut the copy into sections, assemble, illustrate, and create a picture book, a bulletin board, or a mural.

The *Nanny Goat and Her Kids* has appeared in many forms and at many locations. Students could write or audiotape their own versions. At the end of this chapter you will find a list of additional variants, which students could compare to those shared above. See also Eric Kimmel's *Nanny Goat and the Seven Little Kids* illustrated by Janet Stevens and Tony Ross' *Mrs. Goat and her Seven Little Kids* illustrated by the author. These updated variants utilize skateboards and denim jackets. They provide a direct tie to today's latchkey children who are told never to open the door to strangers.

Response to these three versions of *The Wolf and the Seven Little Kids* by kindergarten students in a Sheltered English Class, a class of students who have very little English facility, yielded rich results. The children, who were Spanish speakers from Mexico, illustrated their reactions and dictated explanations of their pictures to their teacher. In retelling their own versions of the *Wolf and the Seven Little Kids,* their stories were often connected to other folktale motifs—such as the well-known Hispanic folktale, *The Weeping Woman (La Llorona).* Here are a few examples that were told in Spanish and translated to English by their teacher, Michelle Garrett:

- A mother who did not take good care of her kids was tricked by the evil rabbit. He cast a bad spell on the mother for the rest of her life.
- The mom was punished for not taking good care of her goats, so the wolf was sent to eat her babies as punishment.
- The mom called on the water world spirits who came up as lambs on the other bank of the river, which then left the wolf no choice but to go to the river and drown himself for being so mean.
- The rooster-footed devil helped the mama goat save her babies instead of the goat getting them.
- The mother sheep uses a clock to hypnotize the wolf to freeze him in his tracks and save her family.
- A rabbit, who did not listen to the mama, went through the wheel of misfortune on his second time of misbehaving. He was condemned to the eternal triangle.
- The mother lamb tricked the wolf to go into the house and he stayed there 'til he died, with an apple tree in his view to torture him 'til he died.

MORE VERSIONS OF "THE WOLF AND THE SEVEN LITTLE KIDS"

Grimm, J. and W. 1979. The Wolf and the Seven Kids in *Fairy Tales of the Brothers Grimm.* New York: Weathervane Books.

Grimm, J.and W. 1995. *The Wolf and the Seven Little Kids.* New York: North-South Books.

Kimmel, E. 1990. *Nanny Goat and the Seven Little Kids.* New York: Holiday House.

Ross, T. 1990. *Mrs. Goat and her Seven Little Kids.* New York: Atheneum.

Trivizas, E. 1993. *The Wolf and the Seven Little Kids.* New York: Scholastic

Young, J 1994. R*ace with Buffalo and Other Native American Stories for Young Readers.* August House.

PART THREE

A World of Stories

In the following four chapters, I share stories collected from students who came to the United States from nearly every continent—Europe, Asia, South America, Africa, and North America. The countries represented are Azerbaijan, Bosnia, Colombia, India, Iran, Korea, Laos, Mexico, and Somalia. The students, whose ages range from seven to seventeen, attended schools in the Midwest in three different school districts—one urban, one suburban middle class, and one suburban upper middle class.

Folktale types, motifs and classifications are useful tools for scholars and researchers, but are not needed to enjoy this genre. While categories considered here grow out of Aarne & Thompson's classification system (1973), students need to know only a few of the major categories. I simplify them into the four groups: Tests and Tricks, Good and Evil, Gratitude and Revenge, and Tales of Magic.

Because the countries represented here cover a vast cultural and geographic area, they present rich and varied classroom possibilities. The stories can become jumping-off points for many curricular directions in addition to English literacy acquisition. Here we have the opportunity to expand nonimmigrant students' knowledge and understanding of other cultures as we support immigrant students' sense of pride in their cultural heritage.

CHAPTER THREE

Tales of Tests and Tricks

A favorite folktale type, tales of tests and tricks, can be found in virtually every culture. Clever and brave or foolish and cowardly protagonists confirm or surprise us, and are always duly rewarded for their actions. The following tales provide an overview of this folktale type.

The Brahmin and the Goat

Told by Wali, a high-school student from India.

One day a Brahmin received a goat as a gift. He picked up the goat and set out for home, carrying it on his shoulders. Three rogues saw the Brahmin carrying the goat. They were hungry. They wished they could get the goat for a meal.

"That's a nice plump goat," said one of them. "Yes," said another, "It would make a good meal for the three of us. But how can we get the goat? The Brahmin will not give it to us." "Listen," said the third rogue. "I have a plan." The third rogue then whispered into the ears of the other two. The other two rogues laughed. Then all three jumped up and hurried away.

The Brahmin walked on. Now, one of the rogues suddenly came along and stood in front of the Brahmin. "Oh, holy sir," said the rogue very politely, "why are you carrying that dog on your shoulders? Surely to a Brahmin a dog is something unclean. I am surprised to see a Brahmin carrying a dog." "Dog?" shouted the Brahmin. "What are you talking about? Are you blind? This is a goat I have just received as a gift." "Now, don't be angry with me, sir," said the rogue in a calm voice. "I am only telling you what I see. But I'll say nothing more. Please pardon me sir." The rogue quickly went away.

The Brahmin walked on, muttering angrily to himself. A little further along the road the Brahmin met a second rogue. The second rogue looked at the goat and he looked at the

Brahmin. "Oh, holy sir," said the second rogue in a sad voice, "you should not carry a dead calf on your shoulders. You know, it is disgraceful for a Brahmin to carry a dead animal." "Dead animal? Dead calf?" shouted the Brahmin. "What nonsense are you talking? Are you blind? Don't you know a live goat when you see one? This is a goat I have just received as a gift." "Please don't get angry with me, sir," replied the second rogue in a very humble voice. "Carry a calf, if you want to, a dead one or a living one. It does not matter to me. I'll say no more. Please yourself."

On walked the Brahmin. He felt a little worried. From time to time he glanced at the goat. Itwas a goat all right. But very soon he met the third rogue. "Pardon me, sir, " said the third rogue, "but I must tell you that what you are doing is most improper." "Improper?" asked the Brahmin. "What is improper?" "It is not proper, sir, for a holy man to carry a donkey. A Brahmin should not even touch such an unclean animal. You must know that yourself. Put it down, sir, before anyone else sees what you are doing."

The Brahmin was now puzzled. He was too worried to be angry. This was the third man he had met. And each one had seen his goat as something different. First a dog, then a dead calf, and now a donkey! Was this goat, then, a goblin or some sort of demon? Could it change itself every few minutes? Perhaps these men were right, after all. Greatly frightened, the Brahmin flung down the goat and ran home as fast as he could.

The rogue picked up the goat and hurried back to his friends. They were happy at the success of their plan. They had a goat meal.

지혜로운 어머니

아주 먼 옛날, 우리 나라에는 고려장이라는 풍습이 있었다. 고려장은, 일할 능력이 없는노인을 멀리 산 속 토굴에 버려 두었다가, 죽으면 장사를 지내는 풍습이었다.

세월이 흘러도 고려장을 지내는 풍습은 사라지지 않았다. 아니, 오히려 더욱 철저하게 지켜지게 되었다.

고려장이 철저하게 지켜지던 그 옛날, 늙으신 어머니를 모시고 사는, 박씨 성을 가진 사람이 있었다. 인자한 성품에다 높은 벼슬자리에까지 올라 있어, 사람들의 존경을 한 몸에 받는 사람이었다.

The Wise Mother

Told by Sik, a middle-school student from Korea.

Long time ago, from our country, Korea, there was a custom named Go-ryo-jang. Go-ryo-jang was an old custom when a person gets old, people would have to leave that person in a deep forest until the person dies, when they do, people would bury them. Because during that period of time, the whole nation were in very poor situation, and also some people thought old people had no use.

Time passed away, but this custom still didn't disappear. No, it became more strict during this period. That time when the custom was very strict, there was a guy named "Park," with his old mother. Everyone looked up to him because of his great personality, with a high respected job from the government and the nation.

It started few days ago, he couldn't sleep. Even with his high respected job, he had to follow the custom Go-ryo-jang. Every citizen has to follow the custom of the country.

He kept thinking, but not an idea came out of his head.

"There is no way I can do this to my mother. Even if I get in a trouble I couldn't leave my living mother in the forest to die. "All right, then," he thought, "I'll hide her under the floor."

He immediately hid his mother under the floor. Letting his family believe that he followed Go-ryo-jang. He started to serve food to his mother privately. He took his own food and brought it to his mother.

"Mother, forgive me. There is no other choice. Please, I know it's hard, but try to be a little patient" His mother felt more sorry for her son, for all this trouble.

"Mother, don't worry, nobody knows. Don't worry and live long-long. I will tell the King, and put this ridiculous custom away."

"Thanks son, I'm always happy. There is this much light coming in, and you always serve me food, but I always worry about you. Didn't someone who tried to hide their parent get punished last time?

It was this one day. Suddenly an ambassador came from a big country over the north river. That country was cautious of our country expending more and more. They would pick a quarrel if there was any chance. With any chance they will try to show that they were more powerful. But every time our country will respond to them with brilliant ideas.

This time, the ambassador said something that caused the whole nation to shake.

They wanted to have a wisdom contest. We didn't know what kind of trap there might be. But our country couldn't say no, because of the situation.

He took out two same looking horses, and showed them. He said arrogantly, "These horses are a mother and a daughter. You people are to figure out which is which, and you have 10 days to figure this out." The King and all his servants were furious, even Park's heart almost stopped. Both horses looked exactly the same. Even their eyes sparked same. They would never be able to guess. The whole country began to panic. Whenever citizens met each other, they would talk about this. They were full of sighs.

"We are in big trouble, there is only one day left, and there is no one in this country who could possibly figure this out?" The King sighed with a headache. His face looked as pale as they could look. When Park saw this, he thought his heart was going to be ripped apart.

Park came home with face full of worry. When he went under the floor, his mother asked,"Is there any problem? You don't look so good."

"No mother," but he had no chance to fool her. He had to tell her everything. After she heard the story, she looked like she was thinking, and then smiled. She whispered into his ears.

Suddenly, son's eyes got bigger, his mother's wisdom was miraculous.

Next day, in the royal palace, everyone looked at each other silently. The big country's ambassador said with an arrogance attitude, "This is the promised day, who will figure out the question?"

"I will." Park raced up. "I have a favor. Do you, ambassador, know which one is the mother?"

"Of course."

"Then write it down in a little piece of paper. You might argue it's not the right answer, even when I got the right answer."

"All right then."

When the ambassador agreed, Park asked a servant for some hay. Then, one horse came out and started to eat till he was full, then the other horse came out and started to eat. After Park saw this horse, he answered. "This horse is the mother. Even a horse lets her child eat first." The Ambassador was surprised. He could only praise Park's wisdom.

Later, when the King figured out that this wisdom came out of Park's mother, instead of punishing him for hiding his mother, he thanked him.

People then realized humans were useful and precious whether they are old or young. They started to talk about the privileges as a son. At last, the King banished Go-ryo-jang and amended the law to respect their old parents.

The Shadow Story

This story was also told by Sik, a middle-school student from Korea.

Once, a long time ago a man was tired from working hard. He was walking home and the sun was very hot. He came to a house with a big tree. The big tree made a big shadow. The tired man wanted to sit in the cool shadow, so he went to talk to the man in the house.

"I want to sit in the shadow of your tree."

"You will have to buy it from me." said the owner.

"Buy the shadow?" asked the tired man. He thought about how cool it would feel to lie down in that shadow. He gave the owner some money for the shadow. Then he lay down in the shadow and enjoyed the coolness.

But, later in the day the shadow moved to rest on the owner's house. The tired man then moved, too and went into the owner's house. He was so anxious to stay with the shadow, he didn't even take his shoes off when he went inside. The owner's family wanted him out. They wanted to buy the shadow back. But, he didn't want to sell it.

Finally, he did sell it back for a lot more money than he paid for it.

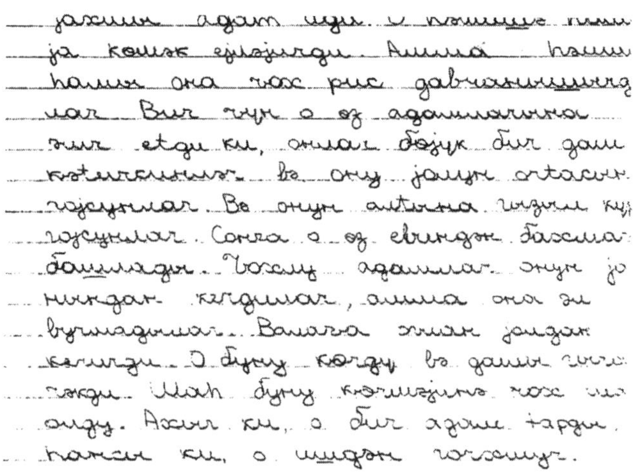

A Stone in the Road

Told by Yegor, a middle-school student from Azerbaijan.

Once there was a village and in this village there was a very rich man. He was a very kind man. He always saw people passing by his house. He always helped them. He had a big fine house. He always asked them to come sit in his house. They were all tired and everything and he invited them to his house to rest and gave them to eat and drink.

This man was a little bit sad, you know, because everyone who passed by was lazy nobody wanted to work or nothing. So, he went home and he thinks and then he decides to order his servants to put a rock in the middle of the road and then he put a pot of gold under it.

So, soon a farmer came by and he said, "Oh, look at this big rock in front of a rich man's house. If I were a rich man I would order my servants to take the rock out of the road!" And he doesn't even touch the stone. He just goes away. And everybody who comes by they don't touch the stone and they say some words and just walk on. This makes the rich man feel sad because no one tries to move the rock.

And much later it's getting a little bit darker. A little guy comes by. He came from work and he's so tired. He sees the rock in the middle of the road. Now he thinks and says to himself, "Now it's getting darker someone could bump into it and fall down." So even though he is tired, he moved the big rock and found the big pot of gold. He couldn't believe his eyes!

At that moment the rich man was looking and sees the little man take the pot of gold, and the rich man is happy now because he found somebody who is not afraid of work, somebody who is kind and thinks of others.

To Find a Wife

Told by Teresa, a second-grade student from Mexico.

Once there was a young man named Jose. He was looking for a wife. When he was out walking one day, he stepped on an ant house and was surprised to hear a scream. It was an ant. He bent down and heard an ant say, "Hey, watch where you walk!" The young man was sorry he had stepped on the ant house, so he built rocks around it so no one else could ever step on it again. The ant said, "Thanks."

As he went on his way he passed a little lake. He heard a voice saying, "Help me." It was a fish trapped under a rock in the lake. He moved the rock and the fish swam free. The fish said, "Thanks."

He went on his way. As he was walking he heard some squeaks. He looked down and saw two baby birds that fell out of their nest. He put them back in their nest. They said, "Thanks."

He went along his way and soon saw a castle. The king in this castle had a beautiful daughter. When the young man saw the king's daughter he wanted to marry her.

The king said, "O.K., but first you must do three things. One: you must pick up all these seeds." Then he took seeds and threw them out into the wind.

The young man thought he would never be able to find them all. But then he heard a voice. It was the ant he had helped. He heard a little voice say, "I will help you." The ant found the seeds for him.

Then the king dropped a ring into the lake and said, "Number two: you must return the princess's ring. The young man thought he would never find the ring in the lake. But then he saw the fish he had helped. In the fish's mouth was something shiny. It was the princess's ring.

Then the king took a necklace and tossed it high on to a tree. "Number three," said the king, "You must bring this necklace back to me." It was up so high that the young man tried, but couldn't reach it. He was about to give up when the baby birds he had helped flew up there and brought the necklace to him.

So, the young man and the princess were married and they lived happily ever after.

CLASSROOM POSSIBILITIES

While these tales of Tests and Tricks provide enjoyment as a simple reading, perhaps the following ideas will stimulate your own creative ways to expand student learning.

Invite students to notice how Tests and Tricks folktales involve a show of bravado, strength, courage, or knowledge in order to fool others, avoid death, and win wealth or a princess. Solving a riddle, slaying a dragon, or tricking the monster saves the protagonist. A familiar, exaggerated example such as *Rumpelstiltskin* further illustrates these qualities. Students can create their own examples, shared orally or in written form.

There are many opportunities to integrate Tests and Tricks into the curriculum. For example, in social studies, the story of the Trojan horse in ancient Greece; in music appreciation, Hayden's Surprise Symphony; and in sports, a championship game.

Who and How

Who and How is a strategy that focuses on characters and their actions as it builds vocabulary. Searching for succinct ways to describe characters and how they act expands the student's vocabulary as it acknowledges the role of characterization in literature. Students brainstorm descriptors to depict their thoughts about what motivates characters to act as they do.that most capture their view of the character's motivations and resulting action. There are many ways to carry out Who and How. The following example, while appropriate for all age groups, was carried out with older students. Here, the use of a Venn diagram provides a visually concise way to broaden vocabulary by describing the characters and their actions in Wali's story, "The Brahmin and the Goat."

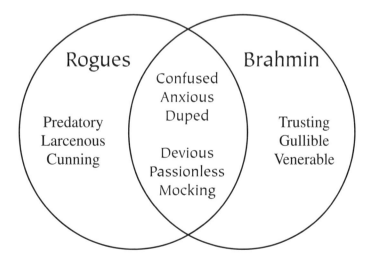

Written Conversation

After hearing or reading these stories, students might consider them more carefully by noting similarities and differences in the exercise, Written Conversation (Burke, 1985). Working in pairs, students think silently about whether each story represented a test or a trick and why. They then write their thoughts to each other without speaking, as if they were having a conversation. The strategy proceeds in the following manner. Two students sit side by side with one piece of paper. They take turns writing their thoughts and responding to each other in written form only. The novelty of not speaking makes this a popular strategy. It is powerful because it not only incorporates the ability to express thoughts in written form, but also requires that their partner's writing be legible and reasonably spelled, thus providing a very practical opportunity to utilize these skills.

Find It

Find It is an approach that calls attention to the countries and cultures represented by the students who told these stories. Two major purposes underlie this strategy: 1) to expand students' knowledge of geographic areas and 2) where possible, to call upon students or guests from the represented countries to share information about these cultures. On a map, identify and locate the countries represented: Korea, Mexico, Azerbaijan, and India. Compare climate, topography, and customs. A simple graphic, such as the example below, can help clarify the concept of continent and the locus of the stories in this chapter.

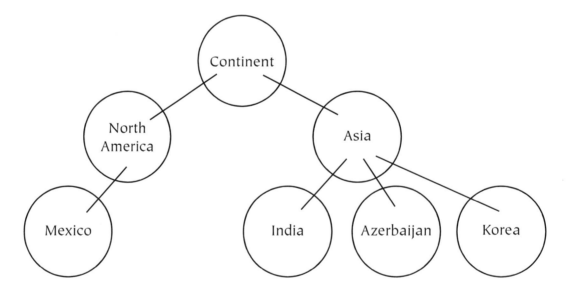

Cubing

Cowan and Cowan developed Cubing to reinforce the material students are studying (Johns, J., 2003). Enjoyed by grade-school and middle-school students, it provides a game-like format for review. Response can take an oral or written form. It has been a useful vehicle for the display of alternative viewpoints. The teacher prepares cubes with a question on each side. The strategy works best if no memory level questions are used, thus allowing for alternative responses. Students are asked to form groups of six. Members of the groups each take turns tossing the cube and answering the question that lands on top. Answers can be given orally or in writing. Others in the group accept or reject the answer given and justify their response. There are many ways to vary this activity. For example, the students in each group could prepare a cube made up of their own questions. The cubes are then distributed among the groups. Thanks to fifth-grade teacher, Susan Gittinger, for her comments and for the following sample:

> Students really enjoyed the cubing activity. We used this often. It provided an easy way to present many of the stories and engage them in conversation. I have attached a copy of one of the cubes we used. As they got familiar with the questions on the cube, the depth at which they approached them really increased. It was also funny to see that they had 'favorite' questions they hoped came up on their roll. One of the most common favorites was, "How would the story change if it happened at [our school]?

This example, when cut and folded, forms a cube:

How would the story change if it happened at our school?	What does this story remind you of?
	How would it change if it happened 100 years from now?
	Who is your favorite character? Why?
How would you end the story?	What was the most exciting event? Why?

MORE TALES OF TESTS AND TRICKS

Carey, V.S. 1990. *Quail Song*. Putnam/Whitebird.

Conger, L. 1970. *Tops and Bottoms*. New York: Scholastic

Cushman, D. 1990. *Possum Stew. New York:* Dutton

Ginsburg, M. 1988. *The Chinese Mirror.* Harcourt Brance Jovanovich.

Goble, P. 1988. *Iktomi and theBounder: A Plains Indian Story.* New York: Orchard.

_____. 1989. *Iktomi and the Berries.* New York: Orchard.

Han, O.S.P. 1993. *Sir Whong and the Golden Pig.* New York: Dial

Hong, L.T. 1991. *How the Ox Star Fell from Heaven.* Albert Whitman

Lester, J. 1987. *The Tales of Uncle Remus*. New York: Dial.

McDermott, G. 1977. *Anansi the Spider: A Tale from the Ashanti.* Holt, Rinehart and Winston.

Mollel, T. W. 2000. *Subira, Subira.* New York: Clarion

Tashjian, V. 1969. *Juba this and Juba that*. Boston: Little Brown.

CHAPTER FOUR

Stories of Revenge and Gratitude

Revenge and Gratitude tales are strong favorites of most children. Their exciting plots (often gory in their earliest forms) command attention, while gratitude tales reassure.

The Little Red Hen

Told by Lorenzo, a first-grade student from Mexico.

A little red hen tried to get some help to make some bread. She asked the donkey and the cat and the dog. They all said, "No." So the hen had to make the bread by herself. When the bread was done, first came the donkey and asked for some bread, then the cat, and then the dog. But, the hen said, "No" to the donkey and the cat and the dog. You know why? Because they didn't help her!

The Lion and the Fox

Told by Yegor, a middle-school student from Azerbaijan.

Once there was a forest and in this forest there lived different kinds of animals. The king of this place is a lion, you know. Once he goes to hunt.

This lion is very kind to every animal. He doesn't eat healthy animals. He eats only sick ones that are going to die. So, he looks and he can't find anything. Then he finds a fox, you know, and he chases him. When he catches him and when he is ready to eat him, the fox says, "Don't eat me!" and those kinds of stuff. You know, a fox is kind of tricky. So, the lion says, "okay."

So, he tells the fox to come and live with him. When the lion catches something to eat, he brings it to table and they both eat. So, once when this lion goes hunting, somebody shoots this lion. When he comes home, you know, he asks for water from the fox. The fox takes a big stone and throws it at the lion.

The lion says, "Why did you do this to me? I've been always good to you."

The fox says, "First when you come, you say, "I have to kill you.' Now, I have to kill YOU!'

So he kills the lion.

The meaning of this story is that in the world it's some people, you know, that even if you are some kind of kindness to them and everything, they will be bad to you.

You can't trust some people

까치와 나그네

어느 날, 나그네가 길을 가고 있었습니다. 그 나그네는 구렁이
가 아기 까치를 먹으려고 하는 것을 보았습니다. 나그네는 화살을 뽑
아 구렁이에게 쏘았습니다. 그러자 그 화살이 구렁이의 가슴에 맞아
죽었습니다.

밤이 어두워 졌습니다. 나그네는 아무데도 잘 곳이 없었습니다.
그래서 집을 찾으려고 하다가 어떤 불빛을 보았습니다. 문을 두드리
자 한 여자가 나왔습니다. 나그네는 "여기서 하룻밤 묵어도 되나요?
잘 곳이 없습니다." 라고 말했습니다. 그러자 그 여자가 말하기를 "그
럼요, 그러나 저 혼자 이 집에 살기 때문에 방에서 나오지 마세요."
그리고 여자는 나그네를 한 방으로 안내했습니다.

The Magpie and the Traveler

Told by Chul, a middle-school student from Korea.

One day a traveler was passing by and he saw a big snake trying to eat a baby magpie. The traveler got his bow and arrow and shot the big snake. The big snake was dead.

When it got dark the traveler didn't have anywhere to sleep. In the woods the traveler tried to find a house but couldn't. While he was trying to find a house he saw a light. He knocked on the door if there was anyone inside and a woman came out. The traveler asked "Can I stay in your house for tonight? I don't have anywhere else to stay." And she said, "Sure, but I only live in this big place so just stay in the room you're staying in." And she led him in to a room.

It was almost midnight; the traveler wasn't in sleep. Something opened the door. When the traveler turned around and looked there was a big, big, fat, long and ugly snake in the room. The snake said, "The big snake you killed with your bow and arrow was my husband. I'll do the same thing as you did to my husband." The traveler said, "Please don't eat me. I swear I didn't know" and then the snake said, "Well, if the big bell rings three times before I eat you in the morning, I'll let you live." The snake thought "Ha! I'm not as stupid as you." The traveler couldn't sleep.

In the morning the snake came into the room. The traveler closed his eyes and thought he was dead until the bell began to ring. It rang three times. The traveler and the snake both said "Whaa, Whaa." The snake left silently.

The traveler went up the hill where the bell was to see who might have done that. When he reached the place he saw a group of magpies dead on the ground. The traveler buried all the magpies and said, "You magpies were braver than me and I'll never forget that." And he left with tears in his eyes.

54

The Leopard's Tale

Told by Gwa, a first-grade student from Laos.

A mother leopard was fighting for people. She eats rabbits. She eats foxes. She doesn't eat people.

A hunter found the mother leopard. He shot her and killed her. He killed the mother leopard. The hunter took it home. He made a coat out of its fur.

The baby leopards were still alive and were taken care of by their father.

The hunter came out again to find the father leopard. The father leopard was brave. He growled at the hunter and the hunter ran away.

But the father leopard caught up to the hunter and killed him.

The babies grew up and became brave like their father. They had no more trouble with hunters. They kept fighting for people like their mother did.

The Lion Story

Told by Yemi, a second-grade student from Somalia.

The lion was king. He killed all the people and said, "I'm king of the jungle!"

He killed with his teeth.

The lion's brother and the queen were friends with all the people in Somalia.

"Get the people back alive," the queen said.

Then the king's brother killed the king, and he put his paws on the people's heart and they all came alive.

The king's baby became king. He was king of the jungle. After that they were friends with all the people in Somalia.

Not for You

Told by Consuela, a third-grade student from Colombia.

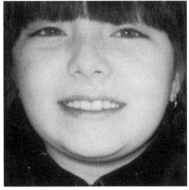

It was a very long time ago that this happened. A long time ago. My grandmother told me. Strangers came to Colombia who wanted gold. People in Colombia then had the gold. But when the strangers asked for all the gold, the people did not want to give it to them because the strangers were mean and bad to them. They wanted all the gold for themselves.

The people decided to hide all the gold. Where to do it?

There was a beautiful lake. It was a very deep lake. They took all the gold and threw it into the lake.

When the strangers came to get the gold, the people in Colombia said their gold had all disappeared. The strangers were angry, but there was nothing they could do. They looked everywhere and found no gold.

The gold was in the lake.

The gold is still in that lake.

CLASSROOM POSSIBILITIES

A brief retelling or reading of a well-known tale of this type will set the stage to explore these stories. For example, *Androcles and the Lion,* a well-known favorite, can quickly connect this story of gratitude to students' experience. Remind students of revenge stories such as the classic, *Snow White.* Briefly discuss the motivation behind the acts of revenge or gratitude seen in *Androcles* and *Snow White.*

Relevance and Synthesis

Relevance and Synthesis (Alvermann, 1986) is a strategy designed to foster critical thinking. Students develop skills in synthesizing and categorizing by learning to recognize and apply relationships. Several sets of terms that relate to commonly known folktales are presented to the class. Each set has four terms, one of which is a nonexample, that is, it does not fit with the others. Once it is found, students identify a generalization that fits the remaining three. Although the following is suggested for young students, Relevance and Synthesis works equally well with those who are older. The teacher could replace this example with one more appropriate for older students. Still, I have seen teachers use extremely exaggerated examples such as these with great success when introducing strategies to older students. If not overdone, they find them amusing and to the point.

When introducing this category to young students, the teacher thinks out loud or demonstrates his/her thinking.

Three Pigs	A Giant	Golden Eggs	Jack

The teacher might say, "Let's see now. One of these things doesn't fit. I know the story of the Three Little Pigs, but I don't think there is a giant in it, or golden eggs, or a boy named Jack. Three Pigs must be the one that doesn't belong because all the others fit the story of Jack and the Bean Stalk."

This strategy stimulates thought. It helps develop a conscious way of reading, rather than mere word-calling, and can help move the reader to consider what was read—a critical literacy.

Here are some possible clusters of terms tied to the stories above.

Bread	A Lady Chicken	Pumpkin Coach	No Helpers [Little Red Hen]
Birds	A Snake	A Big Bell	Magic Apples [Magpies and the Traveler]
A Wolf	A Mother Leopard	A Fur Coat	A Hunter [Fighting for People]
Killing Teeth	A Queen	A Lion	Magpies [The Lion Story]
A Leopard	A Fur Coat	A Lake	A Secret [Not for You]

The Reason Why

The Reason Why is a variation of the *pourquoi,* or explanation, tale. This tale type, a constant throughout the ages, provides creative answers to curiosity about the nature of things and the way things function. Here we can provide students the opportunity to convert Tales of Revenge and Gratitude into tales that explain. Having read the previous stories, the students can consider the motivations behind the characters' actions. This activity requires a grasp of the characters and their basic traits. Having the students elaborate on their explanations in written or oral form can lead to deeper understandings.

Students work with a partner to explore possible explanations for details and actions in the stories. They then compile an outline of a possible explanation for observed action or anticipated action if the story were to continue. They could record their explanation tales on audiotape or write them for others to hear or read.

An example that could tie directly to a social studies consideration of South America's colonization could come from *Not For You* by Consuela. Here, again, responses could take form as drama, dance, poetry, mystery, etc. The following example shows possible questions that students could ask in response to the prompt: Where did the people's gold come from?

- What did it mean to them?
- Why did they have so much gold?
- How did they use it?
- What kind of strangers were these that would make the people forfeit all their gold rather than give it up?
- Who were these strangers and how did they treat the people?

Mandalas

The concept of a mandala has evolved over the ages as a way to express a complex concept in visual form. Utilized by Jung (1964) to explain a *collective subconscious,* the mandala is an image that often depicts a fundamentally meaningful view or belief.

Claggett and Brown (1992) present the mandala as an approach that stimulates response to literature. They work with high-school students, but this strategy has been successful with middle-school students as well. The mandala holds exciting potential for use in classrooms. This strategy gives students the opportunity to express visually what they may not be willing or able to express in oral or written form. It provides a viable way to reach the visual learner. The mandala helps students analyze and organize thoughts and move from the concrete to the abstract through the use of metaphor. Students take the theme of a tale and depict it in a drawing with a phrase written within the picture or along the edge to form a frame. The use of metaphor plays a vital role in establishing a strong connection between the reader and the work of literature. Metaphor expands students' critical and analytic thinking. Because representing their thoughts visually opens an expressive door for students who may have difficulty expressing themselves in words, this would obviously be a welcome option for students whose first language is not English.

After reading one or the entire series of Tales of Revenge and Gratitude, students draw images that represent one tale's basic theme—its overall message. Or, they can focus on the major characters. Mandalas can remain as simple as this, or they can expand for older students. The following example illustrates a possible way to utilize this strategy.

One could pose the story of Cinderella in what Claggett & Brown call a "Sun-Shadow" mandala. Students draw a circle split in half with one half designated "Sun," or positive images; the other, "Shadow," or negative images. This provides a graphic way to address the dualities often found in literature and the possible transformations of characters.

Students could focus on two characters; for example, Cinderella and her stepmother. They then consider what animal, plant, color, natural element, and personality most represents these characters. Students draw these similarities on the circle without using words. Utilizing the metaphors depicted, students then write or tell sun or shadow sentences to represent the images. These sentences are written along the perimeter of the circle to form a frame. For example, "Cinderella is most like the sun because, like the sun, she has a bright outlook." "The stepmother is most like a storm because, like a storm, she brews bad things." To continue the example further, a chart similar to the one below could be constructed for students' responses.

Sun Shadow Mandala

	Sun		Shadow	
1	2	3	4	5
	Most Like	Adjective Describing Column 2	Opposite Of Word In Column 3	Most Like Column 4
Animal	Bunny	Trusting	Suspicious	Snake
Plant	Rose	Gentle	Harsh	Poison Ivy
Color	Bright	Shiny	Dark	Rough
Personality	Trusting	A Bright Outlook	Expects the Worst	Suspicious
Natural Element (Wind)	Summer Breeze	Caressing	Destructive	Tsunami

This represents a powerful vocabulary builder. Students select terms from the chart to construct a sentence that describes the story's theme or characters. For example:

"Like a rose, soft and gentle, Cinderella faced her stepmother, a snake of a woman, whose destructive and rough nature suspected everyone."

They could work in pairs, individually, or within groups to construct a sentence that they write around the perimeter of the circle; then draw these images within it.

MORE TALES OF REVENGE AND GRATITUDE

Climo, S. 1995. *Atlanta's Race: A Greek Myth.*New York: Clarion.

De Beaumont, M.L. 1986. *Beauty and the Beast.* Potter.

Grimm. J.L.K. 1979. *Sixty Fairy Tales of the Brothers Grimm.* New York: Weathervane.

Heyer, M. 1986. *The Weaving of a Dream.* Viking Kestrel.

Hutton, W. 1991. *The Trojan Horse.* McElderry.

Kimmel, E. 1995 *Rimonah of the Flashing Sword: A North African Tale.* New York: HolidayHouse.

Knugson, B. 1990. *How the Guinea Fowl Got Her Spots: A Swahili Tale of Friendship.* Caroirhoda.

Langtoron, J. 1992. *Salt.*New York: Hyperion.

Shepare, A. 1995. *The Gifts of the Wali Dad: A Tale of India and Pakistan*. New York: Atheneum.

Stevens, J. 1989. *Androcles and the Lion*. New York: Holiday House.

Well, R. 1996. *The Farmer and the Poor Good: A Folktale from Japan*. Simon and Schuster.

Yep, L 1990. *The Shell Woman and the King*. New York: Dial.

CHAPTER FIVE

Tales of Magic

Magic inhabits many folktales and plays a central role in the next four stories. When in a powerless position, when it appears that nothing can explain happenings or change the course of events, magic saves the day. Magic is there to transform, resolve, and give hope.

```
Once up on a time
on a sunny day there
lived mom and her son.
On one day the mother
trowed out seeds of
beans and a big bean tree
growed big up to the sky
and mom send him to
go up to the sky, and if some-
body starts chaseing you
down the bean tree
```

Geck and the Bean Stem

Told by two students from Bosnia: Zina, a middle-school student, and her brother, Zulfo, a third-grade student. This version is a compilation of the two versions.

Once up on a time on a sunny day there lived a mom and her son. They lived in a small house. They were poor. One night they were cleaning some beans and threw the bad ones out the window. When they woke up the next day, there was a bean stem with a lot of beans that grew up to the sky. Mom sent him to go up to the sky. "If someone starts chasing you down the bean tree, I am going to dig a hole in the ground so you will fall into it. And now, go!"

The boy went up to the tree and climbed it up to the sky. When he got there he saw a house in front of him. He went there and met a friendly mom giant and she told him that the dad giant is angry on everybody and that he is going to eat the boy if he sees him. Poor child hid, but when the giant came he smelled him and started searching for him. After a long search he found him. The boy started running and made it.

The boy went back the next day and instead of running after giant started chasing him, the boy grabbed a chicken that laid golden eggs. He ran down the stem and told his mom to get an ax ready for him to use. The giant jumped down and fell into the hole that the boy's mother dug out. The mom and her son put dirt in the hole and covered the giant. The giant died. The boy took the ax and cut the bean stem down. Mom and son lived happily ever after.

Diamonds and Snakes

Told by Zina, a middle-school student from Bosnia.

A girl. Her mother dies and her father marries again. Then he dies. The girl has to live with her stepmother and stepsister. The stepmother thinks she is prettier than her daughter so she makes her do all the dirty jobs, makes her clean and do everything.

Once she goes to the place to get water, a pitcher of water. An old lady comes there. She is a fairy godmother, but she is dressed like an old lady. The old lady asks for a drink of water and the girl fills up the pitcher nicely and gives her to drink. The old lady was so glad that she told the girl that when she talks, diamonds would go out of her mouth.

The girl gets home and starts to talk, and her stepmother sees all the diamonds coming out of her mouth. She gets jealous and she sends her daughter there. Her daughter doesn't want to give the old lady anything to drink. So, the old lady said that when the daughter talked, she would have snakes come out of her mouth when she talked. Then the stepmother punished the girl who now talked with diamonds because she thought the girl had lied.

The girl ran away in the woods. A prince saw her and thought she was pretty so they got married and lived happily ever after.

The Magic Apples

Told by Yegor, a middle-school student from Azerbaijan.

A long time ago it's a king and he has three sons. In his garden it's an apple tree and in that apple tree there are apples that when you eat them you get younger. This king needs the apples. One of those guys, the brothers, they see that there are no apples in the tree and they know that somebody is stealing the apples. So they decide that the older one should stay on guard to see who steals, but he falls asleep. And the middle one, he does the same thing. But the younger one, he cuts his finger and puts some salt in there so with his finger hurting he wouldn't sleep.

In the dark after midnight, a big monster comes and steals the apples. The younger son put some mud under the tree so when the monster walks away he can see his footsteps. He follows and finds a big cave with rooms in it. He sees the monster has a girl there. When the younger son sees her, he loves her. He kills this monster and frees the girl.

He puts the magic apples in his pocket for safekeeping and comes home. There he tells his brothers about it. They want to see the girl so they go to the cave. Outside the cave is a well. When they get there, the older brothers say they are thirsty and want some water. The younger brother says, "I'll go in the well and get you water." He gets the water and when he starts to come up, the older brothers cut the rope and he is stuck there a long time. He doesn't know what to do.

An old man comes by and says, "Hey, son, what's your name?" And he says, "I'm ('somebody'—Alex, I think. I forgot his name.)" The old man says, "There will be two ships coming to get you out of the well.

"Ships? I'm in a well. Where are ships?"

"Swim down to the bottom of the well" said the old man. "You will see it turns into a river. There you will see two ships – one black and one white. You get on the white one so you can go to the White World. Don't go with the black one. It goes to the Black World."

The younger brother jumps on the white one, but when he does, a big wave comes up and he gets thrown over to the black one. The black ship takes him to the Black World where everything's black. Everything is dark here. People wear black and people are crying and everything. He asks, "What happened?" And they tell him a big monster has taken all their drinking water. The monster doesn't let drinking water to come there. So the younger brother kills this monster. The king of the Black World asks him to come see him.

On the way, the younger brother sees a snake going up a tree to eat Eagle's babies. The younger brother kills this snake. And the Eagle and the bird babies say, "Thanks. What can we do for you?" The younger brother is surprised they can talk. He says, "Take me to the White World." The Eagle says, "I will, if you give me 40 pieces of meat and 40 pieces of water."

"Where can I find 40 pieces of meat and 40 pieces of water?"

"Go to the king of the Black World and ask for it."

When the younger brother gets there, the king of the Black World is pleased he killed the monster so he says, "You can marry my daughter for killing that monster." But the younger brother says, "No, I am in love with another. But I would like 40 pieces of meat and 40 pieces of water." The king of the Black World agrees.

Then, going back to the Eagle, the younger brother asks for a ride to the White World. The Eagle says, "Climb on my back. When I say, 'give me a piece of meat,' give me a piece of meat. When I say, 'give me a piece of water,' give me a piece of water."

They fly off. And the Eagle gets meat and water when he asks for it. But for the last piece of meat. It falls down. So, there is no more meat to give the Eagle, so, the younger brother cuts a piece of meat from his leg and gives it to the bird. When the bird tastes this meat, it knows this meat is different because it tastes so sweet. The Eagle doesn't eat this meat, but puts it under his tongue to hold it there.

When they get to the White World, the Eagle flies down and lets the younger brother off his back. But, the brother cannot walk on the leg where he cut off a piece of meat. The Eagle takes that meat from under his tongue and puts it back on the brother's leg so he can walk now. The brother says, "Thanks."

Then the Eagle gives the brother three feathers and says, "If you need me just send me one of these feathers." The brother says, "Thanks." The Eagle flies away.

So, the younger brother looks around the White World and sees that everyone is happy, you know.

All this time he has kept the magic apples safe in his pocket.

When he gets home, he sees that the older brother and the middle brother want to marry the girl that the younger brother wants to marry. They are fighting about this.

The younger brother blows one of the Eagle's feathers away and the Eagle comes and asks what he wants. "I want a suit of armor to fight my brothers for the girl." He puts the suit on and fights his brothers and kills them. When the girl sees him she remembers him.

Then the king, his father, comes. When the younger son takes off his hat, the king sees that he is his youngest son. He is very happy because his other sons told him the younger son was killed by a wolf. This was a lie.

The king is so happy his youngest son is not dead that he embraces him.

Now, his son takes the apples out of his pocket and gives them to his father.

"My magic apples!" says the king as he embraces his son once more.

So, the king's son and the girl marry and live happily ever after.

The Angel Who Couldn't Fly

Told by Sik, a middle school student from Korea.

Once an angel, a single guy, was down from heaven. He went to the woods when there was a full moon. He wanted to take a bath, so he took off his clothes. These clothes were full of flying magic. He had special clothes with magic that made him able to fly. When he was in the water someone ran away with his clothes. It was a young woman. She hid his clothes. Now he was stuck because he couldn't fly back to heaven.

He met this young woman and married her. They had children and were happy.

Even though the woman had hidden his flying clothes, her children found them and when they put them on they flew up to heaven. They were sad for their mother, so a flying horse came down and took their mother up to heaven to be with them.

The man was lonely without his wife and children. He prayed for a way up to heaven.

The flying horse could not come down for him because once, when the mother was making soup for dinner, she spilled hot soup on the horse, and the horse then ran away.

So the man prayed some more. This time a bucket came down from the sky and he rode in it to heaven.

This angel and his family were happy together.

CLASSROOM POSSIBILITIES

You could begin a discussion of magical tales by first sharing some contemporary examples. Quickly list and ask students to share knowledge of *Indiana Jones, Superman, Batman, Harry Potter, The Lord of the Rings* or others that have appeared recently on TV, in movies, and computer games. A brief reference to the magical objects or transformations found in these examples helps establish focus for the topic. The class could then consider what situations required magic, how the magic happened, and what affect it had.

The Plausible Impossible

Consider introducing The Plausible Impossible, a concept suggested by Walt Disney. Magic tales that seem most believable, despite the fact that they could never really happen, are the ones that seem most effective. When cartoon characters in flight run off a cliff, hang there momentarily before dropping, and land without a scratch, we know it could never happen. Yet, it doesn't interfere with our enjoyment of the story. We suspend disbelief.

Students could apply this concept to the tales of magic shared above. For example, in Zina's "Diamond and Snakes," the good stepsister is so good and so mistreated that the idea of diamonds coming out of her mouth is perfectly acceptable. By the same token, the bad stepsister is so bad and so unjustly coddled that the idea of snakes coming out of her mouth is also perfectly acceptable. The idea that the diamonds and snakes could be a metaphor for the way people talk would be worth considering. Some people speak such beautiful words that they might be as sparkling as diamonds, and some people speak such ugly words that they might be as menacing as snakes. Perhaps students could share examples of poets, historical characters, or perhaps some people they know.

Say Something/Do Something

After students have had a chance to read one of the stories, the teacher could reread it aloud. As it is reread, the teacher should stop periodically and invite responses to the reading. Students find this Say Something/Do Something strategy, suggested by Barbara Lindberg (1988), a favorite. The idea here is to solicit a brief response—a word spoken, an image acted out or drawn. All age levels enjoy this activity, particularly if it moves quickly and spontaneously.

This strategy provides a risk-free opportunity for students to respond in a medium that is comfortable for them, thus alleviating possible student anxiety about using incorrect English. The teacher could model a response, for example, by sketching a memory the story triggered, raising a question, or using gestures to give a personal opinion.

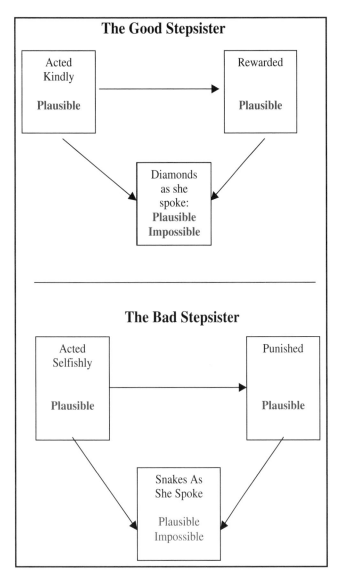

The Good Stepsister

Acted
Kindly

Plausible

Rewarded

Plausible

Diamonds
as she
spoke:
Plausible
Impossible

The Bad Stepsister

Acted
Selfishly

Plausible

Punished

Plausible

Snakes As
She Spoke

Plausible
Impossible

Say Something/Do Something would work well with Yegor's "The Magic Apples." After selecting logical stopping places, the teacher invites the class to draw or jot down comments as she reads. She also models the type and brevity of comments for the strategy. Possibilities include contributing a brief word or two, performing an action or gesture, or simply holding up a drawing in progress. No one makes comments about student contributions during the reading so as not to intrude upon the flow of the text. One possibility would have students seated in a circle. Identify one as the first who will say or do something. After the reading begins, the teacher proceeds around the circle and continues to read and stop until all students who want to participate have had a turn.

An alternative for this strategy is a variation of Story Box (Wendelin, 1991). Put a ball of string or yarn that has knots tied at irregular intervals inside a box with a small hole in the top. When the teacher stops reading, the first student pulls the string and speaks or acts until coming to a knot. Then the student passes the box to the next person in the circle while the teacher continues to read. At the next stop, the second student begins to pull the string, talking and/or acting until s/he reaches another knot.

Following this exercise, the class discusses the story, the comments, and the actions given around the circle. Students consider if and how their view of the story may have changed as it progressed and as others responded. Some possible questions to consider are the following:

- What magic appears in this story?
- What does the magic accomplish?
- Who is effected by the magic and how?
- In what ways do you agree or disagree with other students' responses? Why?
- What do you think makes this story believable? Unbelievable?

Retell

Retell is a strategy developed by Hazel Brown and Brian Cambourne (1987). This seemingly simplistic strategy offers strong learning potential.

Often used with younger students, it is effective with all age levels. Rosen had great success with this strategy when working with high-school students in London (Rosen, B., 1988). The process of restating what has been read (or heard) involves many skill levels. Expanding to written retellings offers even more. Some possible vehicles for receiving and retelling include: oral to oral retelling; oral to written retelling; oral to drawn retelling; written to written retelling; and reading to oral retelling.

This strategy provides intensive language use around a central theme. It develops recall of sequence and plot, and often recaptures style and language use that fits characterization. Retelling invites reflection regarding others' retellings and in revisiting the original text.

After students read the magic tales or hear them read, the strategy could proceed in a number of ways, depending on the students' age level. The teacher could begin before the story is read. S/he could arrange the class into small groups and ask for predictions about the plot based on the title only. They might predict possible words and phrases, characters, and action. After listening or reading the story, the students separate into groups and collaborate on a retelling without consulting the original story. Their retellings could be written out, sketched, pantomimed, or outlined. Following this, groups could share their retellings and justify the directions their versions take.

Guesses about the impact of the oral tradition—of retelling folktales over the years, their travels, and transformations—could follow.

Another Point of View

Another Point of View invites students to tell a story they know and then retell it from the point of view of a character who plays a major role, but who was not prominent in the original story. This calls for the application of imagined response to the plot, using voice and action that would match those of the character represented. Having Another Point of View gives students the opportunity to display their knowledge of characterization and of a particular character's response to the plot. It can demonstrate students' ability portray a story in a new way which is consistent with the theme. Through invented dialogue, the student expands his/her ability to use language for particular purposes.

The Tales of Magic lend themselves well to this strategy. Students select a character in, for example, Indira's "A Fairy Tale," and tell the same story from another character's point of view—perhaps the mean, rich woman or the daughters who can't afford to go to school. Another example is Sik's "The Angel Who Could Not Fly." Here, students might focus on the young woman whose children found the magic clothes and tell her experience of the tale. Or in Zina's "Diamonds and Snakes," the story could be told from the point of view of the fairy godmother, the mean stepmother, or the ugly stepsister.

Students could pair up and select a character that they feel could become more active in the plot. Next, they rewrite or retell the story including their chosen character's thoughts and motivation for new action. Then, students share and discuss these new versions with the class. The class considers how believable the changes are, based on the quality of fit with the original tale. For example, would it be in character for the mean, rich neighbor to invite the beggar lady into her house and feed her before knowing that she might benefit from it? Students explain and justify the direction their rewrites have taken.

Retellings can take many forms. They could be written, danced, drawn, constructed, or spoken. These can grow into an effective culminating activity to the study of magic tales as a presentation to other classes or to a Parent's Night event.

Here are some examples of responses to the "Angel who Couldn't Fly" from one character's point of view written by fifth graders.

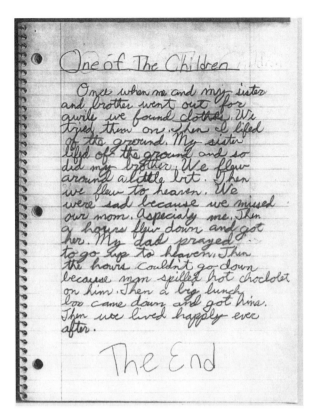

One of the Children

Once when me and my sister and brother went out for a while we found clothes. We tried them on. Then I lifted off the ground. My sister lifted off the ground and so did my brother. We flew around a little bit. Then we flew to heaven. We were sad because we missed our mom. Especially me. Then a horse flew down and got her. My dad prayed to go up to heaven. Then the horse couldn't go down because mom spilled hot chocolate on him. Then a big lunch box came down and got him. Then we lived happily ever after. The End.

I Am a Horse

I was just laying in heaven and then some kids came flying to heaven. It was my job to greet whoever came into heaven. So, I said, "Hi" and showed them to their room. Two weeks later I heard them crying. I asked what was wrong because no one was supposed to cry in heaven. They said they missed their mom. So, I flew down and got her. They were all happy. Two days later the mom was making soup It smelled so good, so I went over. I scared her and she dropped some hot soup on my hoof. You don't know this, but if something hot drops on a flying horse's foot, he can't fly anymore. Two days later they were all crying. So, I asked them what was wrong. They said they missed their dad. So, I said that my best friend would get him. So he did. They all were so happy. Heaven was back to normal. They all lived happily ever after. The End.

Imagine That!

Imagine That! is a strategy that provides students the opportunity to express themselves in a visual, written, or role-playing format. This is particularly useful for students who are unsure of their ability to speak or write in English, whether they are ELL students or not. Invite students to draw their image of a character, a setting, or a point of a view. The picture could be a simple illustration of the story, or it could offer alternative images. For example, following a reading of Yegor's "The Magic Apples," students could make comparative images of the White World and the Black World. They could construct a portrait of the younger son dressed in his armor, depict him lost in the well, on the back of the eagle, etc. Another picture possibility might be that of the king before and after he eats a magic apple. Then they might respond to several questions tied to their pictures—the number and complexity of the questions to be based on their age level and English competence. They could write their answers, write a simple caption, or answer questions orally. If writing anything proves too challenging, they could respond orally, act out their responses, or respond with another picture. The following are possible question ideas:

- *Why do you suppose the White World was so happy?*
- *Describe the monster in the Black World.*
- *Why did he need so much water?*
- *How did he sound, move, and act?*
- *How do you think the Black World might have changed after the monster was killed?*
- *Why do you think the monster came to the Black World instead of the White World?*
- *How do you think the people of the White World might have acted if the monster had come there?*
- *Why do you think the king needed the magic apples? How did he change after eating one of the apples?*
- *Could the White World and the Black World be metaphors for some real world experience?*

MORE TALES OF MAGIC

Cleaver, E. 1985. *The Enchanted Caribou*. New York: Atheneum.

Esbensen, B. J. 1989. *Ladder to the sky*. Boston: Little Brown.

Goble, P. 1984. *Buffalo Woman*. Bradubury.

Haley, G. E. 1986. *Jack and the Bean Tree. Crown*.Crown.

Hodges, M. 1989. *The Arrow and the Lamp: The Story of Psyche*. Boston: Little Brown.

Moroney, L. 1994. *The boy Who Loved Bears: A Pawnee Tale*. Children's Press.

Shetterly, S. H. 1991. *Raven's Light: A Myth from the People of the Northwest Coast.*New York: Atheneum.

Stewig, J. W. 1991. *Stone Soup.* New York: Holiday House.

Uchida, Y. 1993. *The Magic Purse.* McEderry.

Yolen, L. 1978. *Shape Shifters.* Seabury.

CHAPTER SIX

Tales of the Good and the Bad

Stories of the Good and the Bad find devoted fans among young people. It is always reassuring to see that the bad receive proper punishment and the good proper reward. Typically, the characters lack complexity. They appear straightforwardly and consistently good or bad, with no need for a game card to identify the villain or hero. All cultures seem to favor tales of goodness and badness, lies and deceit, and reward and punishment. As these tales play out basic human weaknesses and strengths, they provide a vicarious outlet for their audience. The following immigrant students' stories present no exception. They illustrate the extremes people can find in themselves and others.

To Sing a Song

Told by Sik, a middle-school student from Korea.

Once there were twin brothers, one was good and one was bad. Each was born with an ugly growth on his face. This made life hard for them because they were often teased and called names. Their father said, "Do not let this sour your life. You are healthy and you are smart. You can show others how kindness can give you a full life."

The good brother became sad and quiet. When he did speak, he was kind and cheerful.

He would sing a song to all who he met—those who called him names and those who didn't. Because he had a beautiful voice, everyone who heard him smiled and thanked him for his song.

The bad brother became sad and quiet. When he did speak, he was mean and sullen. He would shout back ugly remarks to all who called him names. He even got into fights with people who did nothing to him but look at him strangely. He was angry all the time. "Don't be so angry, son." their mother said to the bad brother. "Your brother has found something beautiful about himself—his voice. Perhaps you, too, can find something beautiful about yourself."

"I don't sing! And even so, I don't feel like singing!" said the bad brother.

Once the good brother went into the woods to find firewood. When he had a big pile of wood, he wanted to go back home. But, he didn't know which way to go. He had wandered so far into the forest that now he was lost. He put his load of wood down and sat under a big tree to think of what to do. As he sat there he began to sing. As always, his voice was beautiful. It was so beautiful that birds stopped their singing to listen.

Because he was thirsty, he went to a well nearby to drink. He sang another song as he drank. Then, accidentally, he dropped his ax into the well. A Spirit came out of the well and asked, "Who is that singing? " When the good brother said he was singing, the Spirit wanted to know how he could sing so beautifully. "My mother says it's because of this growth on my face."

The Spirit showed the good brother a golden ax. He asked, "Is this your ax?" The good brother said, "No that golden ax is not mine." Then the spirit showed him a silver ax. "Is this your ax?" he asked. The good brother said, "No, that one is also not mine." Then the spirit showed him the ax that had fallen into the well. It was old and dingy. "Is this your ax?" he asked. "Yes. That is my ax," said the good brother.

The Spirit then removed the growth from his face.

The Spirit said, "Your beautiful voice comes from your goodness, not from the growth on your face. Anyone who sings so beautifully should have a beautiful face to go with it." The good brother reached up and touched his face. It was true! The growth on the good brother's face had disappeared. When the good brother tried to thank him, the spirit only wanted to hear another song. And it was true, the good brother could still sing beautifully. Then the spirit guided the good brother out of the forest. The good brother ran home singing for joy.

His brother was not happy to see that there was no growth on the good brother's face. He asked how it happened that now it was gone. When he heard about it, the bad brother set out to the woods to find the Spirit and to have his growth removed, too. He had never tried to sing, but he felt sure he could do it, if his brother could.

It wasn't long before he was deep in the woods. He found the well and dropped his ax into it. Then he sat down near the well and began to sing. But! Such a bad sound he made! His singing was just awful.

Soon the Spirit came saying, "Who is making that awful noise?"

The bad brother said, "Me. I'm singing. Please remove my growth as you did for my brother."

"Just a minute," said the Spirit, "Is this your ax?" It was the golden ax that he showed.

"Yes, yes!" lied the bad brother. "That is my golden ax."

"No, it is not!" said the Spirit. "First, you make awful singing sounds. Then you ask that I remove the growth from your face, and then you don't tell the truth. This is your ax." And he showed the old, dingy ax that the bad brother had dropped into the well. "It's your badness that makes you sing so bad."

Instead of removing the bad brother's growth, the Spirit put another growth on his face! The bad brother now had two growths instead of one.

He tried to sing all the way home thinking that perhaps if he practiced, his singing would improve, and the Spirit would take the growths off his face. But, instead of singing, his voice sounded like groans and wails. The sounds he made kept getting worse and worse. People stuck their heads out of their windows holding their ears and saying, "Please, please stop that awful noise!"

When the bad brother got home, he stayed in the attic away from everyone. And, that's where he lived for the rest of his life.

But, the good brother lived a happy life singing and helping people.

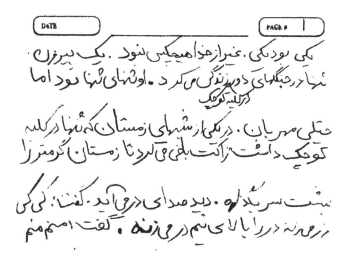

No Room in the House

Told by Rena, a fourth-grade student from Iran.

Once upon a time there was an old woman. She was very poor and she lived in a small house.

One day it was raining very hard and the old woman was sewing and she had her fireplace on, and when she was sewing, she heard a knock on the door. She said, "Who is it?" The cat said, "Mew, mew. It is me, the cat. May I sleep in your house tonight because of the rain. I'll leave tomorrow morning?" The old lady was so kind, and so she gave the cat her bed to sleep on. Then she started sewing again.

Then in a few minutes after, the doorbell rang. She said, "Who is it?" The sheep said to the woman, "It is me, the sheep. May I come and sleep? It's raining so hard. I'll leave tomorrow morning?" She gave the sheep a place, too.

And then more and more came until her whole house was full and she did not have any more room for herself. She had to sleep outside.

Mohalam

This story is also told by Rena, a fourth-grade student from Iran.

During the holiday called Mohalam, people in Iran remember. They remember by wearing only white or black. They remember a sad time when there was a war and the enemies were cruel. The people rode their horses into the desert where one of their enemies trapped them and kept them from having water. The people were very thirsty, especially the children.

Three men tried to talk with this enemy. First, Amam Hassan went to them to ask for water for the children. "Please give us enough water for the children. They are suffering so." But the enemy did not give him water. They shot him with arrows and killed him.

Then Amam Hassaine tried to talk with this enemy. "Please give us enough water for the children. They are suffering so." But the enemy did not give him water. They shot him with arrows and killed him.

And then, Aman Ali tried to talk with this enemy. "Please give us enough water for the children. They are suffering so." Again the enemy did not give him water. They shot him with arrows and killed him.

Finally, a very brave woman, Fatima, went to talk to the other enemies who were in a nearby castle. She bravely made a speech to them and convinced them not to join in with the cruel enemy. They believed her and they broke away from the bad enemy. So the children did have water.

And that's why we remember Mohalam.

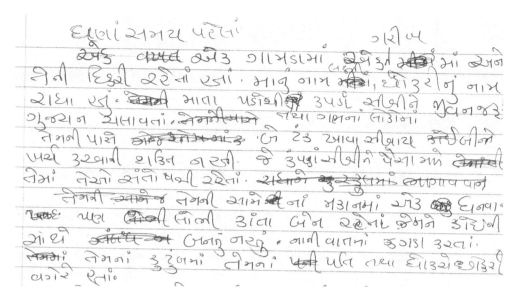

A Fairy Tale

Told by Indira, a high-school student from India.

Once upon a time there lived an old widow with her two daughters. She was very poor and had hardly any money to spend for her house requirements. To run her house and her family she had to sew saris and sell them to her friends and neighbours. She also stitched and repaired clothes of other people and also stitched and repaired clothes that other people gave her instead of paying her. Her daughters couldn't get an education because of the money the schools were asking.

Next to this old widow lady lived a rich and cruel lady. She was very mean to the widow lady because she was poor. She also had two daughters who were just like her.

Once there was an old poor lady who was a beggar who was passing by the rich woman's house. She was hungry and asked the rich lady for some food. The rich lady lied that she didn't have any food and pushed her back and threw her on the ground. Then the poor lady went to the old lady's house who sews clothes, and she asked for some food, too. Since she was kind, she gave her the food that was left with her. Seeing the poor lady's kindness and honesty, the beggar gave her a gift: to wish anything that she wants. But the old widow lady said, "I have everything, I don't want anything." The beggar wanted to give her a gift of her own choice, but since she didn't wish anything, she told her that whatever she did in the

85

morning is what she will do for the rest of her life. Then the beggar left as if she was an angel who had come to give a gift to an old, poor, honest lady to make a living.

Next morning when she got up and started on her sewing, the first thing she did was open her closet and take out a sari. This process didn't stop. It was probably the gift that the old lady had given her. She kept taking one sari after another out of the closet! The poor widow was surprised. Where did these saris come from? After a few hours she was tired, so her daughters helped her. When this incident went into the ears of the rich lady, she was surprised, too. She went to her and asked who or how did this happen. The poor widow told her everything. Next day the old lady passed through that street again and when the rich lady saw her, she called her up and told her that she had some food today, if she would like to eat. The old lady went and ate whatever the rich lady gave. She made sweets and good other dishes. The old lady was surprised. After the old lady was done eating, she started to head out when the rich lady asked her to grant her the same gift that she granted the widow. Since she ate at the rich lady's house, she gave her that gift.

Next morning when she got up she had only one thing in mind—that was to do something that would make her rich. She was about to get up from her bed when she accidentally spilled all the cotton out from her pillow and began sweeping it all up. As the old lady had said, whatever she did or touched is what she would do the rest of her life. So she kept emptying her pillow cotton and sweeping it up. This process made her poor.

The kind and honest widow lady became rich.

DATE 3/25/8   CRVENKAPICA   PAGE 1

*Jedan dan bila jedn djevoj-
ica ime joj je bilo Crvenkapica
Njena mama joj rekla da odne
se nekolko kolačica u korpi
do njene nanu, u putu ona
uturčala u šumu, i ona je
bila uzimala cvječe do puta
do njene nane. Ona se izgub
se poslje, i vuk iskočio i
hodo ispred od nje, i pitoj
gdje ti ideš, i Crvenkapica re
ja idem do moje nane kuče
zato što ona je bolesna
danas, i ja nosim njoj poklon
sa kolačima, i malo cvječa, a
ja sam se izgubila ja nemogi
naći moj put do njene kuče.
Ona zaplaka! Vuk reče, ti m*

Little Red Riding Hood

Told by Zulfo, a third-grade student from Bosnia.

Once up on a time there was a little girl named Little Red Riding Hood. Her mom told her to take some cookies, biscuits in a basket, to her grandmother. Along the way, she ran in to the woods and she picked flowers along the way to her grandmother. She got lost later and a wolf came out and walked in front of her. The wolf asked, "Where are you going?" The Little Red Riding Hood said, "I am going to my grandmother's house because she is feeling sick today. I am bringing her a gift with cookies, biscuits, and some flowers. But, I'm lost. I can't find my way to her house!" She cried. The wolf said, "You can go up the hill there to the right and straight and you will be there. I will go this way and we will see each other up there, okay?"

Later the wolf came first to grandmother's house. Little Red Riding Hood was not there. He went inside to grandmother's bed, and he ate her. He put grandmother's clothes on and got inside the bed.

Later, Little Red Riding Hood got to the house. She knocked on the door. The wolf said, "Come in." Little Red Riding Hood came in. She looked at the bed and the wolf on the bed. She asked, "O, what big ears you have!" The wolf said, "So I can hear you better, my dear." "Oh, what big eyes you have!" said Little Red Riding Hood. The wolf said, "So I can see you better, my dear." "Oh, what big teeth you have!" said Little Red Riding Hood. The wolf said, "So I can eat you!" He jumped up.

Just then a woodsman came by and cut the wolf and took the grandmother out. Then he put rocks and balloons in his stomach and tied the wolf up.

All the people celebrated.

CLASSROOM POSSIBILITIES

Consider leading the class in a brainstorm activity about all the demons, monsters, and bad guys they may have read about or seen on TV; in video games, or at movies. Solicit an alternate list of heroes, angels, and good guys. Typically, students prefer the bad guys. A brief discussion of why we seem to love these "baddies" as much or more than the "goodies" might follow. What purpose do these extremes of character and action represent?

A great opportunity to reinforce the concept of the universality of folktales lies with the story by Sik who is from Korea, "To Sing a Song." It parallels a Nigerian tale, *The Flute* retold by Chinua Achebe. See the Appendix, Tales from Africa, for the citation.

Alternate Discourse Forms

To encourage personal involvement with text, consider offering students the opportunity to respond to the stories in different formats. This approach, Alternate Discourse Forms (Harste, Burke, & Short, 1988), can expand students' understanding of the story as it creates new avenues of expression. For example, students, working in small groups or individually, could take the narrative form of a story and reformulate it into a poem, newspaper article, or radio news report. They could voice the thoughts of the protagonist or of a lesser character. They could turn the story into a television news item or a play. By the same token, they could reformulate it into a clay sculpture, song, dance, or painting. This strategy assures that students have a chance to *express* their responses in a variety of ways, and at the same time, it enhances their ability to *receive* meaning from what they have read or heard. It addresses alternative intelligences through options in the visual arts, drama, dance, and music, as well as the written word.

Thanks to middle school teacher, Lisa Ramey, for the following example that grew out of a discussion of the Taliban's treatment of women. Three students in her class used Rena's story of Mohalam in a TV skit that involves three actors.

Television Interview with Two Women from Afghanistan

(The news reporter begins):

Reporter: Ladies and gentlemen, we have here two Afghanistan women who have agreed to talk with me about how the Taliban have treated women.

What do you think of the way you were treated by the Taliban?

Let me ask the younger lady first.

Young Lady: Well, the treatment was awful. We were not allowed to go to school, to work or even to show our face or to walk alone on the street without being punished terribly.

Reporter: Why did they do this?

Young Lady: Our religion says women are to be modest, but Taliban went too far with this.

Reporter: What punishment would happen?

Young Lady: Well, they would stone us. They would arrest us.

Reporter: (Asking the older lady) Is this the way women have always been treated by people of your religion?

Older Lady: No, sir. Not at all. Our women have been modest without all that. There is an ancient tale about a woman who was so respected because she saved her village where men weren't able to.

Reporter: Really! Tell me about it, please.

Older Lady: Yes. She lived in Iran , but they had the same religion. Her name was Fatima.

(Older Lady tells the story of Mohalam).

Reporter: Thank you both for talking with me. This is Peter Jennings talking to you from Afghanistan signing off.

Question-Answer Relationship

For another possible avenue of response, have students consider the *sources* of answers to questions about the tales. Awareness of the source of information that one reads is crucial to acquiring the skill of critical reading. The Question-Answer Relationship (Raphael, 1982) helps students focus on the location of answers to questions. Most students devote their energies to looking in the text for answers to questions rather than considering where the answer comes from. Unfortunately, because literal questions dominate most school discussions, students often come to expect to find answers appear verbatim in the text. What teacher hasn't heard the frequently expressed student frustration, "I read every single word of the story and the answer is not there!" As a result, asking students to "read between the lines" or to make a judgment on their own about what they have read can be painful—for both teacher and student. Question-Answer Relationship challenges students to explore sources that are

- text explicit ("right there")
- text implicit ("think and search")
- script or schema implicit ("on my own")

Students can learn to reach beyond concrete, memory-level responses to questions. Useful in all phases of the curriculum, this strategy has particular value in the study of literature, since reader interpretation is basic to establishing character or theme.

Because many students will find seeking sources of answers a new experience, a careful introduction can assure success. Modeling the strategy before their first attempt with an exaggerated example would be helpful. You might use a familiar tale, such as *The Three Little Pigs*. "Why did the first little pig's house of straw fall down?" (Text explicit—"right there." The story actually read, "I'll huff and I'll puff and I'll blow your house down!") "Why did the wolf have to climb down the chimney to get to the third little pig?" (Text implicit—"think and search." The wolf couldn't blow down the third little pig's house because it was made of brick.) "Why did the wolf want to capture the pigs?" (Schema implicit—"on my own." Although the story never said so, we know that wolves like to eat pigs.)

Let's apply this approach to Sik's story, "To Sing a Song."

Why do you think one brother could sing beautifully and one could not?

(Text Implicit/ 'think and search').

"What did the Spirit want from the good brother for fixing his face?

(Text Explicit/ 'right there').

"Why did the bad brother stay in the attic the rest of his life?"

(Schema Implicit/ 'on my own').

Story Impressions

Story Impressions provides another approach option. Here, we aim to help students make assumptions *before* hearing or reading a story based upon clues selected and given by the teacher. Developed by Bligh (1995) and McGinley & Denner, (1987), this strategy encourages students to see connections embedded within the story. By looking at a set of clues taken directly from the tale, students identify possible interrelationships among characters and their motivations, which could explain theme or plot. For our stories, it encourages the application of basic folktale knowledge. Before students read one of the tales above, the teacher selects excerpts and makes a list of clues that appear in or out of sequence with the plot. The students work in pairs or small groups to construct a logical story line. Since they base their decisions on general expectations for a folktale, the teacher might first review basic folktale characteristics. (See page 20) Students share their versions with the class. They then read the original to see how closely their version and the original matches.

For example, the following clues could be used for Indira's "A Fairy Tale."

- A poor, but good seamstress and two daughters
- A rich and cruel neighbor
- A beggar lady with magic powers
- One wish to be granted.

Additional Thoughts

Compare Rena's story, "No Room in the House," to Margot Zemach's Jewish tale, *It Could Always Be Worse* (1977). Compare Sik's story, "To Sing a Song," to Chinua Achebe's *The Flute,* a Nigerian tale in Francilia Butler's *Sharing Literature with Children* (1977).

A Writing Triangle

A Writing Triangle (Lloyd-Jones, et al., 1997) is a strategy that clarifies and reinforces the purpose of one's writing. Choosing the appropriate mode of writing will help assure a successful composition. The triangle helps students keep their writing focused

The teacher or the student selects one of the three modes of writing that best fits the writer's purpose. The Expressive Mode is effective when the writer's personal opinion or feelings are emphasized. The Explanatory Mode focuses on describing a process. The Persuasive Mode looks to convince the reader. The Expressive mode is writer-oriented, the Explanatory Mode focuses on the subject, and the Persuasive Mode is the audience-oriented.

A Writing Triangle

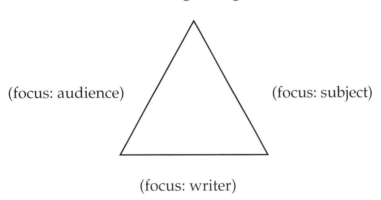

(focus: audience)   (focus: subject)

(focus: writer)

Response to the stories in this chapter could include writing the following:

1. a persuasive piece that features Fatima seeking help to save her people (*Mohalam*)
2. an explanatory piece clarifying the Spirit's thoughts about each brother (*To Sing a Song*)
3. an expressive piece that shows how the poor woman (or the rich woman) felt (*A Fairy Tale*)

MORE TALES OF THE GOOD AND THE BAD

Ada, A.F. 1999. *The Three Golden Oranges*. New York: Atheneum.

Beck, M. 1989. *Heroes and Heroines in Tlingit-Haida Legend*. Anchorage, Alaska: Northwest Books.

Burkert, N.E. 1989. *Valentine and Orson*. Farrar, Straus and Giroux.

Creswick, P. 1984. *Robin Hood*. New York: Scribner.

Delamare, W. 1992. *The Turnip*. Godine.

Ishi, M. 1987. *TheTongue-Cut Sparrow*. Dutton.

Pushkin, A. T. 1998. *The Tale of the Dead Princess and the Seven Knights*. Moscow: Moscow Progress Publishers.

Robin, M. 1988. *The Outlaws of Sherwood*. New York: Greenwillow.

Schroeder, A. 1994. *The Stone Lion*. New York: Scribner.

Yep, L. 1995. *Tiger Woman*. Bridge Water.

PART FOUR

Making Our
Own Folktales

Part Four invites students to create folktales. Here they can get a glimpse of how tales that originate in the oral tradition are shared—first orally, then in written form. They are encouraged to tap their life experiences for meaningful family and cultural stories, material possessions, and/or images recalled or photographed. Through this process, they have the opportunity to strengthen their English speaking, writing, listening, and writing skills.

CHAPTER SEVEN

Come, Tell Us a Tale

This chapter explores ways for students to create folktales. A number of specific suggestions follow. As always, feel free to adapt them to assure they fit the need, age level, and interest of your students. A quick review of basic folktale characteristics will be useful here also, (see p. 20).

Creating our own folktales may seem too daunting a task when we recall their history and the rich cultural influences that gave them birth. It helps to remember that each folktale had to have started somewhere, that at some point some one person or group of people formulated the essence of a tale, and that, over time, it survived its many retellings and variations before reaching us.

Let's jump right in and prepare to experience the joy of making folktales our own.

CLASSROOM POSSIBILITIES

Storytelling

Because folktales originate in the oral tradition, it is only logical that making folktales would start with Storytelling. Wherever possible, students should be given the opportunity to tell their tales. The idea is to foster a relaxed atmosphere—to tap the natural tone and familiarity that is characteristic of oral exchange. Working with a partner or in a small group provides an instant audience and reduces the stress of telling stories in front of larger groups.

Here is a great opportunity to capitalize on students' natural ability to use oral language. Even the youngest students have a vast knowledge of and experience with talking. Unfortunately, it is less common for them to have permission to talk very much in school. Too often student talk in school becomes relegated to a discipline issue, rather than a strong resource for language development. I suggest we take advantage of students' natural ease with oral language. ELL students could tell stories in their first language. They could tell them to others who speak both English and their language for translation into English. For the English-only speaker, hearing the sound of another language broadens an appreciation and knowledge of another culture.

Because there is a difference in usage between oral language and written language, shaping stories into written form calls upon a new set of skills that can be delayed until the joy of story telling takes hold. A carefully planned, introductory lesson can set the tone.

Beginnings

Beginnings is a strategy that should help break the ice. Soliciting a real experience, person, place, event, or thing usually sparks an original folktale. After reviewing characteristics of folktales, encourage students to imagine how to achieve a "folktale quality." (Here again, refer to the list of basic folktale characteristics on page 97) The class could start by working together on a group tale. The teacher poses one story idea and solicits contributions from the class. Done quickly with more attention to plot than detail, it serves to demonstrate the process. The sample should reflect the group's interests and age level. Here are some possibilities to start things off:

- The teacher could look through his/her desk and find: a beanie baby—the main character in a Hero Tale.
- A Good and Evil tale could center around two imaginary rock bands.
- For Tales of Tests and Tricks, perhaps an alien has e-mailed the teacher announcing his arrival in twenty-four hours to destroy the Earth unless a riddle can be solved.
- Team players feel officials were unfair in the way they called the final seconds of a game gone into overtime, causing the team to lose, a possible Revenge Tale.
- A Gratitude Tale could grow from the following idea. Riding the bus to school every day, Jim notices an old man sitting in a doorway. One day Jim decides to get off the bus and talk to the man. The man is hungry and his shoes are worn out. Jim buys him a hamburger at a nearby McDonalds. The next day he gives him a pair of his old running shoes. The man puts a stone in Jim's hand—a stone that he says has magical powers.

Once students accumulate experience creating stories from found objects and imaginary situations, they are prepared to enjoy some of the following story building options.

Story Buddies

Story Buddies, a strategy reported by Nancy Duncan at the National Storytelling Conference in Kansas City in July of 1998, holds extraordinary potential. Her enthusiasm for the procedure and its results were so contagious that I asked for—and received—permission to share it with you. This is an intergenerational community project suggested for students in grades five through twelve. While it does require time to set up and organize, the results are well worth the effort.

The students are paired up with a senior citizen. The senior story buddies share memorable stories about their lives when they were about the same age as the student. Students work on their senior's story for the next three days, and on the fifth day, the senior citizens are invited back to school to hear their stories retold to the entire group. Retelling a story directly from its source gives students an authentic experience in story making. When they apply general characteristics of folktales to their retelling, students develop an understanding of and appreciation for the genre. They develop language ability and confidence. The result is a real-life connection with the community and its history. At the same time, it gives senior citizens direct contact with schools in a positive, powerful way.

For best results, this strategy should probably follow a unit on folktales to assure a general knowledge of the medium. Arrangements are then made with senior citizens who are active; that is, able to attend two school meetings. Invitations are sent directly to potential senior citizen story buddies or to the administration of a nearby retirement home, describing the purpose and schedule of the project.

The projected timeline for the this exercise is as follows:

- Day One: At school, buddies meet and sit together in the classroom. Seniors tell a five-minute story of a memorable event or happening when they were about the same age as their buddy. The story is told three times and after each telling, the student retells it.
- Days Two, Three, and Four: Students retell the story frequently, at home and at school. They make story maps and illustrations. Props are not really necessary but can be used if they enhance the telling. Teachers and students give feedback to help shape the stories and make them as effective as possible.
- Day Five: The senior citizens return and pair up with their buddies. A performance of the stories then follows.
- Afterwards: The follow-up for an event of this type can lead in many directions. Presentations, either video- or audiotaped, provide a repeatable record for both senior citizens as well as the children. Student-made booklets of the written retellings with illustrations make exciting contributions to the school library. Newspaper and television coverage can promote positive community relations. Possibilities that grow out of the experience can enrich the curriculum. This experience often provides the best kind of motivation for student interest in history, geography, and culture. Perhaps students can reap the greatest benefit from utilizing *story* to become acquainted with the lives of people in their community who are from another generation (and possibly another culture).

Template Tales

Template Tales provides another approach that helps stimulate the creative process. Template Tales are tales that evolve from characteristic patterns. All age groups can utilize this strategy and apply it at various levels of complexity. It has been particularly successful with ELL students because the guidelines are so concrete. Invite students to create a tale based on a given template that incorporates basic components of a folktale type. Variations can include modern day as well as traditional settings, situations, and characters. Here students call upon their creativity to apply characteristics of folktale types in a patterned format. With a partner or in a small group, students work within the boundaries of a template to create a new story. Steps in the templates need not follow a particular sequence. Rather, the focus of this strategy rests on the overall structural type. Students share several quick oral versions of a template before deciding which one they write, illustrate, and share with the class.

Template #1 Impossible Tasks
- A person
- An impossible task
- The reason for the task
- The helper who has a secret
- The helper's price
- How the secret is discovered
- What happens to the helper

Template #2: Capture and Escape
- Two children
- Why they leave home
- How they get lost
- How they meet a witch or monster
- How they are trapped
- How they escape
- Their life afterward

Template #3: Foolish Wishes
- A man or woman
- A supernatural character
- An encounter
- The man or woman's spouse
- Two silly wishes
- A third wish to undo the first two wishes

Template #4: The Unlikely Hero
- Three people
- One of them appears foolish

- A king or queen
- A task
- A reason for the task
- Two normal appearing people fail to solve the task
- Foolish appearing person succeeds
- How this is accomplished
- The happy ending

Family Stories

Many students find the Family Stories strategy a favorite. A natural curiosity about students' very own personal histories fuels this approach. Immigrant students' families represent one of the strongest resources for connecting diverse cultures. However, numerous obstacles can come into play when trying to arrange parent participation—parent work schedules, embarrassment about the use of English, and unfamiliarity with our schools, to name a few. Nevertheless, this rich resource need not be overlooked. One way to avoid this difficulty is to structure the exercise so that visiting the classroom is an option. For example, family members could share their stories without leaving home by enlisting the help of a neighbor or relative who speaks both English and their first language.

Wherever possible, connecting school knowledge to personal knowledge pays strong dividends, and personal histories provide a natural vehicle to make this connection. A simple retelling of family stories can lend a missing taste of meaning to an immigrant student's schoolwork and a valuable extension of understanding to nonimmigrant students. Of course, let's not forget that nonimmigrant students also tap their personal histories by tracing their grandparents, great-grandparents, or great-great-grandparents' stories of coming to the United States. Personalized descriptions can make far-off places come alive. For example, (only if families agree) they could describe their country of origin; recount their reasons for immigration to the United States; and give descriptions of the travel involved, the early days of settlement, and present day family locations. (See the Appendix for a bibliography of stories about immigration experiences.) This is potential "pay dirt" in establishing bridges between nonimmigrant and immigrant students. Because of the skills involved, perhaps intermediate and older students are most appropriate for this strategy. However, younger students can gain much from family stories adapted to fit their interests and skill levels.

The following example comes from Lorenzo, a first-grade student, whose mother wrote this description of Mexican history in both English and Spanish.

En la region montañosa
de Nayarit, Mexico se
encuentran dos grupos
de Indigenas llamados
los Coras y los Huicholes.

Estos dos grupos de
Indigenas fueron como
quien dice la cuna
de la Nacionalidad
Mexicana.

Hoy en día existen
pequeños grupos
que siguen con sus
mismas tradiciones
en vestimentas,
religiones, y platós
típicos.

In a mountaenous region
of Nayarit Mexico there
can be found, two groups
of Indian Peoples. These
groups are known as the
Coras (Kōr-ahs) and the
Huicholes (Wē-chō-lěs).

These two groups of India
are the Ansestors of the
nation of Mexico.

Until this day these India
groups live by the traditi
of their forfathers. There
Clothing, Religion & typica
diet remain unchanged.

In a mountainous region of Nayan't, Mexico, there can be found two groups of Indian peoples. These groups are known as the Coras (Kor-ahs) and the Hvicholes (We-cho-les). These two groups of Indians are the ancestors of the nation of Mexico.

Until this day, these Indian groups live by the traditions of their forefathers. Their clothing, religion, and typical diet remain unchanged. The clothing is hand woven from cotton fiber employing many different colors. Grain is the stable of their diet. My son, Lorenzo, and I are happy for this opportunity to share a small piece of Mexican History.

Unlike the previous example, where the parent wrote in both languages, the child in the following example has written her parent's story in English:

Hello, Rita, Thank you for the notebook and the pen. I want to tell you a story from my country. Colombia is a beautiful country very rich in minerals, variety of plants and animals. Has a beautiful weather during all year, the winter there is different. We don't have snow, but it rains a lot. We have very friendly people. Thank you. I'll see you in a few weeks.

Shared family experiences often yield meaningful stories or details that can grow into stories. Tracing these travels and experiences holds potential for integrating all areas of the curriculum, particularly geography, history, and the arts.

By building strong connections to personal knowledge we can establish a strong model for school learning. Students learn to plan and carry out interviews, organize and analyze data from which to compose stories, and learn of the heritage of classmates whose backgrounds are similar and/or different from their own. In addition, this strategy provides reinforcement and application of literacy skills.

Travelogues and Travel Bags

Another way to tap personal connections for students' tales comes from the Travelogues and Travel Bags strategy. Here, opportunities to share family experiences can come either directly with or without the presence of a family member at school. Students involve their families by taking a traveling book bag or suitcase home. Families add a story and/or a representative item that holds some meaning to them. They contribute a travelogue—a description of their place of origin, their cultural heritage for inclusion in the travel bag. The items and stories collected provide a visual and concrete connection to the diversity represented in the class. Students come into direct contact with their classmates' personal backgrounds. A permanent record in the form of a travelogue, based on information included in the travel bag and composed by the class, provides a practical, meaningful writing project. Each student can take the case home for a weekend to collect stories and possible items to add to the collection. Items might include a book, a recipe, a scarf, candlesticks, photos, songs, etc. (all to be returned, of course). Stories could be audiotaped if writing in English is a problem, or they could be written in their first language and translated orally. Upon returning, the student could design and place a sticker representing their country or state on the travel bag. After each child explains the items that his/her family put into the case, another chapter of the travelogue is completed. Older students can write their own chapters. With younger students, dictation or a group writing project works well. The completed travelogue and display would be a proud addition to the school library.

Material Folklore, that is, tales about inanimate objects, can produce exciting stories.

Tales from Things

The Tales from Things strategy works well with tactile learners who feel more comfortable holding something concrete in their hands as they compose a story orally. Here again, items that belong to the student or the student's family can provide that sometimes elusive, sought-after, strong connection between personal knowledge and school knowledge. Using found objects from home, students create folktales that center around the object. The stories can be true or imaginary, set in the past, the future, or in contemporary times. Students develop creativity and imagination by identifying items that they feel hold strong story potential. This strategy requires application and display of their knowledge of folktale types and characteristics. They develop language skills in the execution of the stories both orally and in written form, as well as in their rationale for the selection. As an audience to classmates' stories, they develop listening and critique skills of identifying and questioning as they give each other feedback.

Students read, or the teacher reads to the class, tales about inanimate objects. They brainstorm possibilities that can be found around the home. Items in a junk drawer work well—a program from a play or a recital, a key, a photo, a postcard, a piece of string, one earring, or a plastic toy. Other possibilities include a baseball mitt, a pressed flower, a candlestick, a receipt, a hat, or one mitten.

Students select two or three possible items to bring to school. They build story maps—that is, descriptive outlines of tales for these items—and share them in small groups. The group sessions provide feedback that help select which could turn into the best story. Once that item is selected, the student polishes his/her tale and meets again with the group to practice telling the story. The story is then told to the class (or perhaps to another class). Videotaped, these make an effective Parents Night program. Their stories in written form become a treasured class book or journal.

Interview

The Interview strategy works best with older students because of the skills it requires. This approach utilizes the interview process at two levels. Once students become acquainted with general interview procedures, they interview each other. This can help develop group coherence and understanding. Students then interview members of their own families to reinforce their family's history and origins. The intent here is for language growth in creating relevant questions, in careful listening, and in recording, organizing, and reporting their findings. Reports take the form of a story that is told or written. This interaction can provide the interviewer a new view of the interviewee's culture. Through discussion and role-play, students gain experience in basic interview tactics. Possible considerations include:

- gain permission to do the interview
- arrange for a quiet place to conduct the interview
- prepare good questions and follow-up prompts
- assure interviewees that they can choose to "pass" on any question asked
- pace the questions
- look at the subject as s/he talks
- listen carefully

• conduct audio- or videotaping sessions, and/or take notes during the interview (with the subject's permission)

Students contact immediate and extended family members to arrange interviews. Some may require telephone calls, e-mail, or postal mail. Attention to what makes for good and not-so-good questions, follow-up questions, and prompts can be as detailed as they are age appropriate. A choice of modes to collect the data can add new dimensions, for example, tape recorders, camcorders, note taking, and/or photographs. Upon completion of the interviews, students sort through the data to identify possible story material. The students can follow the following steps to process the information from the interview:

• make story maps
• try out oral renditions in small groups or with the class
• hear and give feedback to facilitate selection of one version
• polish the first draft
• write the story

Students brainstorm questions and try them out on each other. Some examples: Where did your family originally come from? What is your proudest moment? What was your saddest moment? What was your favorite toy as a young child? Who is your personal hero? In addition, they brainstorm appropriate prompts, such as, "I'd like to hear more about that," "Why do you feel that way?" and "Tell me more."

During the interview they can learn to anticipate the way the interviewee looks and feels. Then, based on their guesses, discuss how to proceed with the interview. The class could construct a graphic organizer such as the M chart below, and list categories in each space. Students could role-play interviews and receive feed back from the observers.

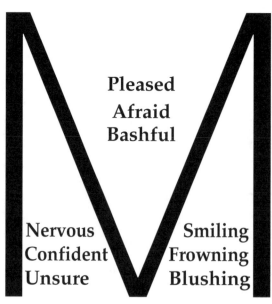

Once the students feel comfortable with preparations such as these, the interviews begin. First, each student interviews another student in the class. Then interviews take place at home, for example, with a parent, grandparent, uncle, or family friend. After the data collection, students organize their findings, construct, tell, and write a story based on each of the interviews. A collection of these stories can form a class album.

Jump Rope Rhymes

Jump Rope Rhymes are invitations for spontaneous creativity that reflect the immediate neighborhood and culture. Favorites for generations, they are a natural outgrowth of play. Old jump rope rhymes delight and amuse us while new ones appear on playgrounds and back yards everyday. Children often match folktale characters and contemporary ideas with the rhythm of the rope. Beresin (1995) found that recently some commercial companies have recognized the drawing power of these rhymes. The McDonalds Company, for example, has sponsored Double-Dutch contests in urban neighborhoods and then printed them as menu charts in local papers, for example, "Big Mac, Fillet Fish, Quarter Pounder, Fries/Ice Coke, Milk Shake, Root Beer Float . . ." The Reebok Company has also used jump rope rhymes in commercials, "Do your foots the Reebok way / Reebok moves are here to stay."

Here is a natural opportunity to demonstrate the poetic quality of sound and rhythm. Jump rope rhymes are not only pure oral tradition, but, as Beresin says, they are kinesthetic and intensely visual" (Beresin, A.,1995).

There are numerous sources of jump rope rhymes. The students themselves are probably the richest resource. Immigrant students can share their versions of rhymes and, if recited in their first language, offer a personal touch to newcomers and an expanded view of another culture to others. The shared informality often yields creative results.

In the following, from *Children' Folklore,* by Sutton-Smith, et al. (1995), students could expand on the original by making up their own variations.

Cinderella	Hello
Cinderella dressed in yellow	Hello, hello, hello, sir.
Went downstairs to kiss her fellow.	Meet me at the grocer.
How many kisses did she give?	No, sir. Why, sir?
One, two, three, four, five . . .	Because I have a cold, sir.
Cinderella dressed in green	Where did you get the cold, sir?
Went outside to eat ice cream.	At the North Pole, sir.
How many spoonfuls did she eat?	What were you doing there, sir?
One, two, three, four, five . . .	Counting polar bears, sir.
Cinderella dressed in lace	How many did you count, sir?
Went upstairs to powder her face.	One, two, three, four, five . . .
How many powder puffs did she use?	
One, two, three, four, five . . .	

The invitation to create new jump rope rhymes can yield surprisingly impressive results. The class can go outside or to the gym, and working in small groups, share the rhymes they know and then branch out creating something new. They can perform them for the class, who later provides feedback. Afterward, they then could write and illustrate their rhymes and bind them into a class book. A videotape of their creations is a natural for a Parents Night program complete with student introductions.

MORE BOOKS ABOUT JUMP ROPE RHYMES, PUZZLES, GAMES, AND OTHER PLAYGROUND CREATIONS

Bayer, J. 1984. *My Name is Alice*. New York: Dial Books for Young Readers.

Booth, D. 1993. *Doctor Knickerbocker and Other Rymes*. Ticknor and Fields.

Cole, J. 1990. *Miss Mary Mack and Other Children's Street Rhymes*. Morrow.

DePaola, T. 1983. *Sing, Pierrot, Sing: A Picture Book in Mime*. London: Methuen.

Hallworth, G. 1966. *Down by the River: Afro-Caribbean Rhymes, Games and Songs for Children*. New York: Scholastic.

Hunter, I. J. , 1977. *Simple Folk Instruments to Make and to Play*. New York: Simon and Schuster.

Langstaff, N. J. 1970. *Jim Along, Josie, A Collection of Folk Songs and Singing Games for Young Children*. New York: Harcourt Brace Jovanovich.

Mattox, C. E. 1989. *Shake It To the One That You Love the Best: Play Songs and Lullabies from Black Musical Traditions*. El Sobrante, CA: Warren-Mattox.

Scruggs, A. 2000. *Jump Rope Magic*. New York: Blue Sky Press.

Winn, M. 1974. *The Fireside Book of Fun, Games, and Songs*. New York: Simon and Schuster.

INANIMATE OBJECT TALES

Achebe, C. 1977. *The Flute* in Sharing Literture with Children, A Thematic Anthology. Waveland Press.

Grimm, J.G. and W. 1978. *The Twelve Dancing Princesses*. Viking.

Haviland, V. 1961. *Why the Sea is Salt* in *Favorite Fairy Tales Told in Norway*. Boston: Little Brown.

Lnag, A. 1981. Alladin and the Wonderful Lamp. Viking..Mayer, M. 1980. *East of the Sun and West of the Moon*. Four Winds.

PART FIVE

Where We Are Now

CHAPTER EIGHT

Summary and Conclusion

Folktales are powerful bridges that connect diverse cultures. The universality of their motifs and messages demonstrate strong commonalities. At the same time, stories told and re-told, read and reread, establish a meaningful link to one's own culture. Here is a double opportunity to reinforce one's uniqueness as well as one's connection to a world of diversity. Folktales can provide a potentially powerful role in our multicultural society.

The multicultural quality of US society expands each year. With the increase of immigrant students in our schools comes the need to give support to regular classroom teachers, as well as support for English as a Second Language programs. It is the regular classroom where the immigrant student spends most of the school day. Few teacher certification programs offer background and/or direct preparation to address the needs of students whose first language is not English. The curriculum presented here represents one attempt to fill this gap.

Stories speak to us. They have staying power. Stories of old have survived political, economic and societal changes. The narrative form captures our attention as few other forms do. It is not surprising, then, that a narrative approach has been identified as an effective vehicle for language learning. Sharing meaningful folktales in both oral and written form can expand literacy levels of all students.

The curriculum presented here builds upon the possibilities imbedded within *story*. It attempts to help establish a level of literacy in English that goes beyond merely calling words or recounting an author's meaning once a passage is read. It aims at being able to relate the meaning of what is read to the reader's life experience and to make a judgment about it. In other words, to establish *critical literacy*, a literacy that enables and encourages taking an active role in a participatory democracy. This aim is as valid for students in the regular classroom, whose primary (or only) language is English, as well as for those who are learning English.

By sharing stories, the curriculum presented in this book has two major aims. One is to expand opportunities for both immigrant and nonimmigrant students to gain knowledge of the culture of others and validation of their own cultural heritage. The other is to move learners toward critical literacy. We can enrich the path to English literacy by recognizing two of our greatest resources: diverse school populations and creative teaching. To teach creatively is challenging work—work that utilizes the powerful learning opportunities diversity provides. Every day teachers address the literacy needs of students with vastly differing cultural and language backgrounds. The No Child Left Behind program (however well-intentioned) intrudes upon this effort in a number of ways, not the least of which limits creative teaching.

The immigrant students who took part in this study attended schools in three different school districts. They came from a wide range of geographic and cultural sites—Azerbaijan, Bosnia, Colombia, India, Iran, Korea, Laos, Mexico, and Somalia. Their stories were audiorecorded in separate interviews and then transcribed verbatim. These stories form the basis for discussion as well as an invitation for those using the curriculum to share their own stories. Suggested instructional strategies incorporate the stories into the language arts, literacy, and social studies curriculum.

The chapter "One Story and its Travels" provides students a striking example of the universality of folktales. Three students who had recently immigrated from cultures as diverse as Korea, Bosnia, and Iran were the source for this tale. Although they had never met each other, they were familiar enough with this tale that, unsolicited, they told virtually the same story.

Twenty stories from the students who participated in this study are organized into clusters of tale types—tales of: Tests and Tricks; Revenge and Gratitude; The Good and The Bad; and Magic. As students and teachers discover similar tales from diverse cultures, rich opportunities to emphasize cultural similarities—as well as distinctive qualities—emerge. By utilizing the numerous strategies that accompany the tales, teachers can support growth in English language literacy.

The final chapter, "Making Folktales Your Own," presents suggestions that help students create tales. Students experience writing and/or telling tales through strategies such as Story Buddies (generational tales), Tales from Things (found object tales), Travelogues (country of origin tales), Template Tales (tales that follow basic folktale formats), Family Stories (personal history tales), and Interview Tales (tales culled from interviews with others).

Maxine Greene reminds us that

> We are appreciative now of storytelling as a mode of knowing . . . of the connection between narrative and the growth of identity, of the importance of shaping our own stories and, at the same time, opening ourselves to other stories in all their variety and their different degrees of articulateness. (1995)

Tales from the Cultures of Students Who Told Stories for This Book

TALES FROM AFRICA

Aardema, V. 1997. *Who's in Rabbit's House?* New York: Dial
———. 1978. *Ji-Nongo-Nongo Means Riddles*. Four Winds
Anderson, D.A. 1993. *The Origin of Life on Earth: An African Creation Myth*. Sites Productions.
Carric, M. 1978. *I Can Squash Elephants*. New York: Viking.
Diakite, B. W. 1999. *The Hatseller and the Monkeys*. New York: Scholastic.
Grafalconi, A. 1986. *The Village of Round and Square Houses*: Boston: Little Brown.
Hamilton, V. 2000. *The Girl Who Spun Gold*. New York: Blue Sky Press.
Kimmel, E. 1995. *Rimonah of the Flashing Sword: A North African Tale*. New York: Holiday House.
Knutson, B. 1990. *How the Guinea Fowl Got Her Spots: A Swahili Tale of Friendship*. Caroirhoda.
Lester, J. 1987. *The Tales of Uncle Remus*. New York: Dial.
———. 1998. *More Tales of Uncle Remus: Further Adventures of Brer Rabbit, His Friends, Enemies and Others*. New York: Dial.
Lottridge, C. 1989. *The Name of the Tree*. New York: McEldemy Books.
Martín, F. 1992. *The Honey Hunters*. Cambridge: Candlewick Press.
McDeermott, G. 1977. *Anansi the Spider: A Tale from the Ashanti*. Holt, Rinehart and Winston.
Medearls, A. 1994. *The Singing Man*. New York: Holiday House.
Mike, J. M. 1992. *Gift of the Nile: An Ancient Egyptian Legend*. Troll.
Mollel, T. 1992. *The Princess Who Lost Her Hair: An Akamba Legend*. Troll.
Onyefulu, O. 1994. *Chinye: A West African Folk Tale*. New York: Viking.
Radin, P. 1952. *African Folktales*. New York Schocken.
Soulhami, J. 1996. *The Leopard's Drum: An Ashanti Tale from West Africa*. Boston: Little, Brown.

TALES FROM EUROPE

Araujo, F. P. 1993. *Nekane, The Lamina & the Bear: A Tale of the Basque Pyrenees.* Rayve Productions.

Diakite, B. W. 1999. *The Hatseller and the Monkeys.* New York: Scholastic.

Gag, W. 1960. *Gone is Gone.* Putnam.

Hastings, S. 1987. *Sir Gawain and the Loathly Lady.* Mulberry.

Jaffe, N. 1998. *The Way Meat Loves Salt.* New York: Henry Holt.

Kellog, S. 1985. *Chicken Little.* Morrow.

Penn, M. 1994. *The Miracle of the Potato Latkes.* New York. Holiday House.

Philip, N. 1992. *Fairy Tales of Eastern Europe.* New York: Clarion.

Rockwell, A. 1986. *The Three Sillies and Ten Other Stories to Read Aloud.* New York: Harper & Row

Sendek, M. 1973. *The Juniper Tree and Other Tales from Grimm.* Farrar, Straus.

Sherman, J. 1993. *Rachel the Clever.* Little Rock: August House.

Singer, I.S. 1966. *Zlateh the Goat and Other Stories.* New York: Harper and Row.

Stewig, J. W. 1991. *Stone Soup.* New York: Holiday House.

Whitney, T.P. 1983. *The Moon-Brothers: A Slavic Tale.* Morrow.

TALES FROM INDIA

Brown, M. 1961. *Once a Mouse.* New York: Scribner's.

De Roin, N. 1975. *Jataka Tales: Fables from the Buddha.* Houghton Mifflin.

Duff, M. 1078. *Rum Pum Pum: A Folk Tale from India.* Macmillan.

Kamal, A. 1989. *The Bird Who Was an Elephant.* Lippincott.

Lestere, J. 2001. *Sam and the Tigers,* New York: Scholastic.

Mehta, L. 1985. *The Enchanted Anklet: A Cinderella Story from India.* Toronto: Limur.

Ness, C. 1996. *The Ocean of Story: Fairy Tales from India.* Lothrop, Lee and Shepard.

Shepard, A. 1995. *The Gifts of Wali Dad: A Tale of India and Pakistan.* New York: Atheneum.

Staples, S. F. 2000. *Shiva's Fire.* Farrar, Straus and Giroux.

Tata, M. 1994. *Favorite Tales from the Panchatantra.* Tata Publications.

Zeman. *Gilgamesh the King.* Tundra.

TALES FROM KOREA

Bercaw, E. C. 2000. *Halmoni's Day.* New York: Dial.

Carpenter, F. 1972. *Tales of a Korean Grandmother.* C.E. Tuttle.

Climo, S. 1992. *The Korean Cinderella.* New York: Harper Collins.

Han, O.S.P. 1993. *Sir Whong and the Golden Pig.* New York: Dial.

Jaffe, N. 1995. *Older Brother, Younger Brother. A Korean Folktale*. New York: Viking.

Huyn, Peter. 1986. *Korea's Favorite Tales and Lyrics*. Seoul: Tuttle/Seoul International.

Rhee, Nami. 1993. *Magic Spring: A Korean Folktale*. New York: Putnam.

McMahon, P. 1993. *Chi-Hoon: A Korean Girl*. Caroline House.

Kim, Helen. 1996. *The Long Season of Rain*. New York: Holt.

TALES FROM SOUTHEAST ASIA

Cha, D. 1996. *Dia's Story Cloth: The Hmong People's Journey of Freedom*. New York: Harper Collins.

Ho, M. 1990. *Rice Without Rain*. Lothrop, Lee and Shepard.

Lichtveld, N. 1994. *I lost my Arrow in a Kankan Tree*. Lothrop, Lee and Shepard.

Livo, N. J. 1991. *Folk Stories of the Hmong*. Englewood, Colorado: Libraries Unlimited,

Xiong, B. 1993. *Nine-in-One Grr! Grr! A Folktale from the Hmong People of Lao*. Children's Book Press.

Shephard, Aaron. 2005. *Adventures of Mouse Deer. Tales of Indonesia and Malyasia*. Skyhook Press.

Kanppent, Jan. *Flowing from the Nine-Headed Serpent*. Washington, DC.

Clark, Ann Nolan. 1979. *In the Land of Small Dragon*. New York: Viking.

Nhuong, Huynh. 1992. *The Land I Lost: Adventures of a Boy in Vietnam*. New York: Harper and Row.

TALES FROM MEXICO

Aardema, V. 1979. *The Riddle of the Drum: A Tale from Tizapin*, Mexico. Four Winds.

Beals, C. 1970. *Stories Told by the Aztecs: Before the Spaniards Came*. Abelard.

Bernhard, E. 1994. *The Tree That Rains: The Flood Myth of the Huicholy Indians of Mexico*. New York: Holiday House.

Bierhorst, J. 1996. *The Monkey's Haircut and Other Stories Told by the Maya*. New York: William Morrow.

Burns, A. F. 1983. *An Epoch of Miracles: Oral Literature of the Yucatec Maya*. Austin: Univeristy of Texas Press.

Gaudiano, A. 1992. *Azteca: The Story of a Jaguar Warrior*. Roberts Rinehart/ Denver Museum of Natural History.

Greger, C. S. 1994. *The Fifth and Final Sun: An Ancient Aztec Myth of the Sun's Origin*. Houghton Mifflin.

Heurer, M. 1983. *El Zapato y el Pez*. Mexico City: Trillas.

Johnston, T. 1996. *My Mexico*. Mexico Mio

Kutyca, M. and Kobeth, A. G. 1984. *Tigers and Opossums*. Boston: Little, Brown.

Rohmer, H. 1982. *The Legend of Food Mountain*. Children's Book Press.
Slocum, M. C. 1965. *The Origin of Corn and Other Tzeltal Myths*. Mexico City: Tlalocan.

TALES FROM THE MIDDLE EAST

Al-Saleh, K. 1985. *Fabled Cities, Princes and Jinn from Arabic Myths and Legends*. Schocken Press.
Burton, R. F. 1977. *Tales from Arabian Nights*. Crown.
Demi. 1987. *Chen Ping and His Magic Axe*. Dodd, Mead.
Kimmel, E. A. 1994. *The Three Princes: A Tale from the Middle East*. New York: Holiday House.
Shepard, A. 1995a. *The Enchanted Storks*. New York: Clarion.
———. 1995b. *Forty Fortunes, A Tale of Iran*. New York: Clarion.
Stanley, D. 1990. *Fortune*. New York: Morrow.
Asian Cultural Center for UNESCO. *Folktales from Asia for Children Everywhere*. Book Five. 1977. Weatherhill.
Conger, David. 1987. *Many Lands, Many Stories: Asian Folktales for Children*. Tuttle.

TALES FROM THE FORMER USSR

Ada, A. F. 1999. *The Three Golden Oranges*. New York: Atheneum.
Afanasev. 1973. *Russian Fairy Tales*. Pantheon.
Bilenko, A. 1974. *Ukranian Folk Tales*. Kiev: Knipro Put.
Chandler, R. 1980. *Russian Folktales*. New York: Random House.
Cole, J. 1983. *Bony-Legs*. Four Winds.
Ginsbert, Mirra. 1970. *Three Rolls and One Doughnut: Fables From Russia*. New York: Doubleday.
Harvey, G. 1995. *Immigrant Girl: Becky of Eldridge Street*. New York: Holiday House.
Hastings, S. 1993. *The Firebird*. Candelwick.
Hodges, M. 1980. *The Little Hump-Backed Horse*. New York: Farrar, Straus and Giroux.
Isele, E. 1984. *The Frog Princess*. Crowell.
Langtron, J. 1992. *Salt*. New York: Hyperion.
McCurdy, M. 1987. *The Devils Who Learned to be Good*. Boston: Little, Brown.
Polacco, P. 1988. *The Keeping Quilt*. New York: Simon and Schuster.
Pushkin, A. T. 1998. *The Tale of the Dead Princess and the Seven Knights*. Moscow: Moscow Progress Publishers.
———. (n.d.). *The Fisherman and the Goldfish*. Moscow: Moscow Progress Press.
Smirnova, G. 1993. *Fairy Tales of Siberian Folks*. Fital.

Winthrop. E. 1990. *Vasilissa the Beautiful: A Russian Folktale*. New York: Harper Collins.

TALES FROM SOUTH AMERICA

Bierhorst, J. 1988. *The Mythology of South America*. New York: Morrow.
Flor, A. 1989. *Feathers Like a Rainbow: An Amazon Indian Tale*. New York: Harper.
Jaramillo, N. P. 1994. *Grandmother's Nursery Rhymes*. New York: Harper.
Kurtz, J. 1996. *Miro in the Kingdom of the Sun*. Houghton Mifflin.
Olivera, F. 1991. *The Woman Who Outshone the Sun: The Legend of Lucia Zenteno*. Children's Press.
DePaola, T. 1980. *The Lady of Guadalupe*.
Loverseed, Amana. 1991. *Thunder King: A Peruvian Folktale*.
Shephard, Aaron. 2005. *The Wings of the Butterfly, Native South American Folk Tales*. Skyhook.

A Cinderella Bibliography

Afanasev (Reteller) (1973). *Russian Fairy Tales.* Ill., Pantheon. (Russia). See "The Golden Slipper"

Clark, A. N. (1979). *In the Land of the Small Dragon.* Chen, B. Ill., Viking. (Vietnam).

Climo, S. (1989). *The Egyptian Cinderella.* Heller, R. Ill., Crowell. (Egypt).

Climo, S. (Reteller) (1992). *The Korean Cinderella.* Helleer, R. Ill., Harper Collins.(Korea).

Climo, S. (1996). *The Irish Cinderlad.* Krupinski, L. Ill., New York, Harper Collins.(Ireland).

Cole, J. (Reteller) (1983). *Bony-Legs.* Ill., Four Winds. (Russia).

Compton, J. (Reteller) (1994). *Ashpet: An Appalachian Tale.* Compton, K. Ill., Holiday. (U.S)

Daly, J. F. (2000). *Brown and Trembling: An Irish Cinderella Story.* Ill., New York, Farrar, Straus & Giroux. (Ireland).

Delamare, D. (1993). *Cinderella.* Ill., Green Tiger Press. (Italy).

Hickox, R. (1998). *The Golden Sandal.* Hillenbrand, W. Ill., Holiday House. (Middle East).

Jacobs, J. (1894). *Tattetrcoats in More English Fairy Tales David Nutt.* Ill. (England).

Jaffe, N. (1998). *The Way Meat Loves Salt.* August, L. Ill., Henry Holt. (European Jewish)

Levine, G. C. (1997). *Ella Enchanted.* Ill., New York, Scholastic. A novelized version

Louie, A.-L. (Reteller) (1982). *Yeh-Shen.* Young, Ed Ill., Puffin Books. (China).

Martin, R. (1992). *The Rough-Face Girl.* Shannon, D. Ill., Putnam & Grosset. (Algonquin, Native American).

Nimmo, J. (Reteller) (1993). *The Starlight Cloak.* Todd, J. Ill., Dial. (Ireland).

Onyefulu, O. (Reteller) (1994). *Chinye: A West African Folk Tale.* Safarewicz, E. Ill., New York, Viking.

Perrault, C. (1965). *Cinderella or the Little Glass Slipper.* Ill., Dover. (France).

Pollock, P. (Reteller) (1996). *The Turkey Girl: A Zuni Cinderella Story. Little Brown.* (Native American).

San Souci, R. O. *Little Gold Star: A Spanish American Cinderella Tale.* Ill., S. Martinez.

Steptoe, J. (1987). *Mufaro's Beautiful Daughters*. Ill., Lothrop, Lee & Shepard. (Zimbabwe).

CINDERELLA PARODIES

Afanasev. 1973. "The Golden Slipper." *Russian Fairy Tales*. Pantheon.

Clark, A. N. 1979. *In the Land of the Small Dragon*. New York: Viking.

Climo, S. 1989. *The Egyptian Cinderella*. Crowell.

_____. 1992. *The Korean Cinderella*. New York. Harper Collins.

_____. 1996. *The Irish Cinderlad*. New York: Harper Collins.

Cole, B. 1988. *Prince Cinders*. Putnam.

Cole, J. 1983. *Bony-Legs*. Four Winds.

Compton, J. 1994. *Ashpet: An Appalachian Tale*. Compton, K. New York: Holiday House.

Daly, J. F. 2000. *Brown and Trembling: An Irish Cinderella Story*. New York: Farrar Straus & Giroux.

Delamare, D. 1993. *Cinderella*. Green Tiger Press.

Edwards, P. D. 1997. *Dinorella, a Prehistoric Fairy Tale*. New York: Scholastic.

Hickox, R. 1998. *The Golden Sandal*. New York: Holiday House.

Jocobs, J. 1894. "Tattercoats." *More English Fairy Tales*. England.

Jaffe, N. 1998. *The Way Meat Loves Salt*. New York: Henry Holt.

Karlin, B. 1989. *Cinderella*. New York: Scholastic.

Lattimore, D. N. 1997. *Cinderhazel, the Cinderella of Halloween*. New York: Scholastic.

Levine, G. C. 1997. *Ella Enchanted*. New York: Scholastic.

Louie, A.L. 1982. *Yeh-Shen*. Puffin Books.

Lowell, S. 2000. *Cindy Ellen: A Wild Western Cinderella*. New York: Harper Collins.

Martin, R. 1992. *The Rough-Face Girl*. Putnam and Grosset.

Minters, F. 1994. *Cinder-Elly*. New York, Viking.

Nimmo, J. 1993. *The Starlight Cloak*. New York: Dial

Onyefulu. O. 1994. *Chinye: A West African Folk Tale*. New York: Viking.

Perlman, J. 1992. *Cinderella Penguine, or The Little Glass Flipper*. New York: Scholastic.

Perrault, C. 1965. *Cinderella or The Little Glass Slipper*. Dover, France.

Pollock, P. 1996. *The Turkey Girl: A Zuni Cinderella Story*. Boston: Little Brown.

San Souci, R. D. 1998. *Cindrillion, A Caribbean Cinderella*. New York: Simon and Shuster.

———. 2000. *Cinderella Skeleton, A Fractured Tale in Rhyme*. Harcourt Brace.

Steptoe, J. 1987. *Mufaro's Beautiful Daughters*. Lothrop, Lee and Shepard.

Wegman, W. 1993. *Cinderella*. Hyperion Books for Children.

American Heritage Tales

Baylor, B. 1976. *And it is Still That Way: Legends Told by Arizona Indian Children*. New York: Scribner's.

Bierhorst J. 1987a. *Doctor Coyote: Native American Aesop's Fables*. Macmillan.

———. 1987b, *The Naked Bear: Folktales of the Iroquois*. New York: Morrow.

———. 1992. *Lightning Inside You and Other Native American Riddles*. Lothrop, Lee and Shepard.

Bowman, J. C. 1957. *Mike Fink*. Boston: Little Brown.

Bruchac, J. 1996. *Between Earth and Sky: Legends of Native American Sacred Places*. San Diego: Harcourt Brace.

Day, E. C. 1989. *John Tabor's Ride*, Edward C. Day.

Durell, A. 1989. *The Diane Goode Book of American Folk Tales & Songs*. Dutton.

Felton, H. W. 1968. *Tall Tales of Stormalong: Sailor of the Seven Seas*. Prentice-Hall.

Freedman, R. 1985. *Cowboys of the Wild West*. New York: Clarion Books.

Johnston, R. 1994. *The Tale of Rabbit and Coyote*. Putnam.

Kellogg, S. 1984. *Paul Bunyan*. Morrow.

———. 1988. *Johnny Appleseed*. Morrow.

———. 1989. *Pecos Bill*. Morrow.

———. 1992 *Mike Fink*, A Tall Tale. Morrow.

Kherdian, D. 1987. *Bridger: The Story of a Mountain Man*. Greenwillow.

Leland, C. G. 1984. *The Algonquin Legends of New England*. Houghton Mifflin.

McDermott, G. 1993. *Raven: A Trickster Tale from the Pacific Northwest*. Harcourt Brace Jovanovich.

———. 1994. *Coyote: A Trickster Tale from the American Southwest*. Harcourt Brace Jovanovich.

Rounds, G. 1949. *Ol' Paul, the Mighty Logger*. New York: Holiday House.

Sackett, S. J. 1967. *Cowboys and the Songs They Sang*. New York: Wm. R. Scott.

Shapiro, I. 1962. *Heroes in American Folklore*. Messner.

Shepard, A. 1993. *Legend of Sloppy Hooper*. New York: Scribner's.

San Souci, R. D. 1993. *Cut From the Same Cloth: American Women of Myth, Legend and Tall Tale.* Philomel.

Spencer, E. 1993. *A Flag for Our Country.* Steck-Vaugh.

Wilson, J. H. 1986. *Justin Wilson's Cajun Fables.* New York: Pelican.

APPENDIX D

Diversity/Immigration Tales

Anno, am. 1990. *All in a Day*. Philomel.

Baer, E. 1990. *This is the Way We Go To School: A Book About Children Around the World*. New York: Scholastic.

Bales, C. A. 1997. *Tales of the Elders: A Memory Book of Men and Women Who Came to America as Imigrants – 1900-1930*. Follett.

Bunting, E. 1996. *Ellis Island*. New York: Holiday House.

Freedman, R. 1980. *Immigrant Kids*. Dutton.

Goble, P. 1980. *The Gift of the Sacred Dog*. Bradbury

Graff, N. 1993. *Where the River Runs: A Portrait of a Refugee Family*. Boston: Little Brown.

Gray, N. 1988. *A Country Far Away*. Orchard.

Hamanaka, S. 1994. *All the Colors of the Earth*. New York: Morrow.

Harris, J. 1985. *A Statue for America*. Four Winds.

Harvey, B. 1995. *Immigrant Girl: Becky of Eldridge Street*. New York: Holiday House.

Hoberman, M. 1994. *My Song is Beautiful: Poems and Pictures in Many Voices*. Little Brown.

Holland, I. 1996. *The Promised Land*. New York: Scholastic.

Igoa, C. 1995. *The Inner World of the Immigrant Child*. New York: St. Martin's.

Kidd, D. 1991. *Onion Tears*. Orchard.

Kindersley, A. 1997. *Celebrations! A Children Just Like Me Book*, UNICEF.

Levitin, S. 1986. *Journey to America*. Macmillan

Lingingston, M.C. 1996. *Festivals*. New York: Holiday House.

Maestro, B. 1996. *Coming to America: The Story of Immigration*. New York: Scholastic.

Pellowski, A. 1982. *First Farm in the Valley: Anna's Story*. Philomel.

Polacco, P. 1988. *The Keeping Quilt*. New York: Simon and Schuster.

Reynolds, M. 1997. *The New land: A First Year on the Prairie*. Victoria, British Columbia: Orca.

Sterne, E. G. 1983. *The Slave Ship*. New York: Scholastic.

Takaki, R. 1993. *A Different Mirror*. Boston: Little Brown.

Tran-Khanh-Tuyet. 1987. *The Little Weaver of Thai-Yen Village*. San Francisco: Children's Press.

Winter, J. 1992. *Klara's New World*. Knopf.

APPENDIX E

Additional Listings

Aesop. 1985. *Aesop's Fables*. Holt, Rinehart and Winston.

Brett, J. 1987. *Goldilocks and the Three Bears*. Putnam

Calmenson, S. 1989. *The Principal's New Clothes*. New York : Scholastic.

Clavino, I. 1980. « *Bella Venezia* » in *Italian Folktales*. New York : Harcourt, Brace Jovanavich.

Clark, M. 1990. *The Best of Aesop's Fables*. Boston : Little Brown.

D'Aulaire, I.I.P. 1962. *The Book of Greek Myths*. Doubleday.

Ernst, L.C. 1995. *Little Red Riding Hood, A New Fangled Prairie Tale*. New York: Scholastic.

———. 2000. *Goldilocks Returns*. New York: Simon and Schuster.

Hamilton, V. 2000. *The Girl Who Spun Gold*. Blue Sky.

Kipling, R. 1978. *Just So Stories*. New York: Weathervane.

Minters, F. 1996. *Sleepless Beauty*. New York: Scholastic.

O'Neal, S. 1999. *Shaq and the Beanstalk and Other Very Tall Tales*. New York : Scholastic.

Scieszka, J. 1989. *The True Story of the Three Little Pigs*. Viking Kestrel.

Silverman, E. 1996. *Gittl's Hands*. BridgeWater.

Sturges, P. 1999. *The Little Red Hen (Makes a Pizza)*. New York: Scholastic.

Trivizas, E. 1993. *The Three Little Wolves and the Big Bad Pig*. New York : Scholastic.

Young, E. 1989. *Lon Po Po*. New York : Scholastic.

Zelinsky, P. O. 1986. *Rumpelstiltskin*. New York: Scholastic.

Folktale Resources

Aarne, A. T., S. 1973. *The Types of Folktales*. Helsinnki: Folklore Fellows Communications.

American Folklore. [web site]. Available: www.americanfolklore.net/folk tales/hh.html-7k 2005.

Bauman, R. P., A.,. 1972. *Toward New Perspectives in Folklore*. Austin, TX: University of Texas Press.

Bettelheim, B. 1976. *The Uses of Enchantment: The Meaning and Importance of Fairy Tales*. New York: Knopf. Distributed by Random House.

Blatt, G. 1993. *High Fantasies in Once Upon a Folktale*. In G. Blatt, ed. New York, New York: Teachers College Press.

Bosma, B. 1992. *Fairy Tales, Fables, Legends, and Myths* (second ed.). New York: Teachers College Press.

Brunvand, J. H. 1968. *The Study of American Folklore*. New York: Norton.

Campbell, J. 1991. *Mythology: Primitive, Oriental, Creative, Occidental*. New York: Penguin.

Campbell, J. 1991. *Mythology: Primitive, Oriental, Creative, Occidental*. New York: Penguin.

Carney, S. 2005. *Folktales: What are they?* [web site]. Available: http://wwwfalcon.jmu.edu/ramseyil/tradecarney.htm [2005.

Conger, D. ed. 1987. *Many Lands Many Stories*. Rutland, VT: Charles E. Tuttle.

Dundes, A. ed. 1983. *Cinderella: A Casebook*. New York: Wildman Press.

Galit Hasan-Rokem & Shulman, D. 1996. *Untying the Knot on Riddles and Other Enigmatic Modes*. New York: Oxford University Press.

Golden, J. M. 2000. *Storymaking in Elementary and Middle School Classrooms—Constructing & Interpreting Narrative Texts*. Hillsside, NJ: Laurence Erlbaum.

Helbig, A. and A.Perkins. 1997. *Myths & Hero Tales: A Cross-Cultural Guide to Literature for Children & Young Adults*. Westport, CT: Greenwood Press.

The History of Folktales. [web site]. Available: http://www.geocities.com/athens/delphi/3603/contnetshtml [2005.

Horneyansky, M. 1980. The Truth of Fables. In Egoff, S., G. T. Stubbs, and L. F. Ashley, eds. *Only Connect Readings on Children's Literature* (second ed., pp. 121-132). Toronto, Canada: Oxford University Press.

Jung. 1964. Man and His Symbols: Dell.

Lourie, H. 1980. Where is Fancy Bred? In Egoff, S., G. T. Stubbs, and L.F. Ashley, eds. *Only Connect: Readings on Children's Literature* (Second ed., pp. 106-110). Toronto, Canada: Oxford University.

Lynn, L. L. 1996. Runes to Ward Off Sorrow: Rhetoric of the English Nursery Rhyme. In Egoff, S.,G. Stubbs, R. Ashley, and W. Sutton, eds. *Only Connect: Readings on Children's Literature* (Third ed., pp. 110-121). Toronto: Oxford University Press.

Lynn, R. N. 1995. *Fantasy Literature for Children & Young Adults: An Anotated Bibliography.* New Providence, N.J.: Bowker.

Mahy, M. 1996. A Dissolving Ghost. In Egoff, S, G. Stubbs, R. Ashley, and W. Sutton, eds. *Only Connect: Readings on Children's Literature* (Third ed., pp. 135-153). Toronto: Oxford University Press.

Norton, D. E. 1999. Through the Eyes of a Child. An Introduction to Children's Literature: Prentice-Hall.

Richmond, W. E. ed. 1957. *Studies in Folklore. In Honor of Distinguished Services of Professor Stith Thompson.* Bloomington, Indiana: Indiana University Press.

Rooth, A. B. 1951. The Cinderella Cycle. Lund: Gleerup, C. W. K.

Stories to Grow By. [web site]. Available: http://www.storiestogrowby .com/ [2005.

Thomas, J. 1996. Woods and Castles, Towers and Huts: Aspects of Setting in the Fairy Tale. In Egoff, S, G. Stubbs, R. Ashley, and W. Sutton, eds. *Only Connect, Readings on Children's Literature* (Third ed., pp. 122-129). Toronto: Oxford University Press.

Travers, P. L. 1996. Unknown Childhood. In Egoff, S., G. Stubbs, R. Ashley, and W. Sutton, eds. *Only Connect: Readings on Children's Literature* (Third ed., pp. 130-135). Toronto: Oxford University Press.

Turner, S. R. 1994. *The Creative process: A Computer Model of Storytelling and Creativity.* Hillside, N.J.: Erlbaum.

Wrightson, P. 1996. Deeper Than You Think. In Egoff, S., G. Stubbs, R. Ashley, and W. Sutton, eds. *Only Connect: Readings on Children's Literature* (Third ed., pp. 154-161). Toronto: Oxford University Press.

Zipes, J. 1984. *The Trials and Tribulations of Little Red Riding Hood.* Hadley, MA: Bergin & Garvey.

Copy-Ready Materials
(For Classroom Use Only)

COMPLETE COPY OF GRIMM'S
THE WOLF AND THE SEVEN KIDS

The Wolf and the Seven Kids

By the Brothers Grimm

There was once an old Nanny-goat who had seven Kids, and she was just as fond of them as a mother of her children. One day she was going into the woods to fetch some food for them, so she called them all up to her, and said—

"My dear children, I am going out into the woods. Beware of the Wolf! If once he gets into the house, he will eat you up, skin, and hair, and all. The rascal often disguises himself, but you will know him by his rough voice and his black feet."

The kids said, "Oh, we will be very careful, dear mother. You may be quite happy about us."

Bleating tenderly, the old Goat went off to her work. Before long, some one knocked at the door, and cried—

"Open the door, dear children. Your mother has come back and brought something for each of you."

But the Kids knew quite well by the voice that it was the Wolf.

"We won't open the door," they cried. " You are not our mother. She has a soft gentle voice; but yours is rough, and we are quite sure that you are the Wolf."

So he went away to a shop and bought a lump of chalk, which he ate, and it made his voice quite soft. He went back, knocked at the door again, and cried—

"Open the door, dear children. Your mother has come back and brought something for each of you."

But the Wolf had put one of his paws on the window sill where the Kids saw it, and cried—

"We won't open the door. Our mother has not got a black foot as you have; you are the Wolf."

Then the Wolf ran to a Baker, and said, "I have bruised my foot; please put some dough on it." And when the Baker had put some dough on his foot, he ran to the miller and said, "Strew some flour on my foot."

The Miller thought, "The old Wolf is going to take somebody in," and refused.

But the Wolf said, "If you don't do it, I will eat you up."

So the Miller was frightened, and whitened his paws. People are like that, you know.

Now the wretch went for the third time to the door, and knocked and said—

"Open the door, children. Your dear mother has come home, and has brought something for each of you out of the wood."

The Kids cried, "Show us your feet first, that we may be sure you are our mother."

He put his paws on the window-sill, and when they saw that they were white, they believed all he said, and opened the door.

Alas! It was the Wolf who walked in. They were terrified, and tried to hide themselves. One ran under the table, the second jumped into bed, the third into the oven, the fourth ran into the kitchen, the fifth got into the cupboard, the sixth into the wash-tub, and the seventh hid in the tall clock-case. But the Wolf found them all but one, and made short work of them. He swallowed one after the other, except the youngest one in the clock-case, whom he did not find. When he had satisfied his appetite, he took himself off, and lay down in a meadow outside, where soon he fell asleep.

Not long after the old Nanny goat came back from the woods. Oh!

What a terrible sight met her eyes! The house door was wide open, table, chairs, and benches were over-turned, the washing bowl was smashed to atoms, the covers and pillows torn from the bed. She searched all over the house for her children, but nowhere were they to be found. She called them by name, one by one, but no one answered.

At last, when she came to the youngest, a tiny voice cried:

"I am here, dear mother, hidden in the clock-case."

She brought him out, and he told her that the Wolf had come and devoured all the others!

You may imagine how she wept over her children.

At last, in her grief, she went out, and the youngest Kid ran by her side. When they went into the meadow, there lay the Wolf under a tree, making the branches shake with his snores. They examined him from every side, and they could plainly see movements within his distended body.

"Oh, heavens!" thought the Goat, "is it possible that my poor children whom he ate for his supper, should be still alive?"

She sent the Kid running to the house to fetch scissors, needles, and thread. Then she cut a hole in the monster's side, and, hardly had she begun, when a Kid popped out its side, and, as soon as the hole was big enough, all six jumped out, one after the other, all alive, and without having suffered the least injury, for, in his greed, the monster had swallowed them whole. You may imagine the mother's joy. She hugged them, and skipped about like a tailor on his wedding day. At last she said:

"Go and fetch some big stones, children, and we will fill the brute's body while he is asleep."

Then the seven Kids brought a lot of stones, as fast as they could carry them, and stuffed the Wolf with them till he could hold no more. The old mother quickly sewed him up, without his having noticed anything, or even moved.

At last, when the Wolf had had his sleep out, he got up and, as the stones made him feel very thirsty, he wanted to go to a spring to drink. But as soon as he moved the stones began to roll about and rattle inside him. Then he cried—

What's the rumbling and tumbling
That sets my stomach grumbling?
I thought 'twas six Kids, flesh and bones,
Now find it's naught but rolling stones.

When he reached the spring, and stooped over the water to drink, the heavy stones dragged him down, and he was drowned miserably.

When the seven Kids saw what had happened, they came running up, and cried aloud—"The Wolf is dead, the Wolf is dead!" and they and their mother capered and danced round the spring in their joy.

(Quoted with permission from *Sixty Fairy Tales of the Brothers Grimm.* 1979. Weathervane Books. Pp 202-205.)

CORRECTED VERSIONS
OF STUDENTS' STORIES

Five Little Goats, Their Mother, and the Big Bad Wolf

Told by Zulfo, a third-grade student from Bosnia.

Once upon a time, there lived five little goats and their mother. They lived in a little house beside the river. On the other side of the river lived a big, bad wolf.

One sunny day mother and her five little ones ran out of food.

The mother told the five little ones not to open the door to anybody until she came back.

Later the wolf came across the river and knocked on the door. The five little goats answered, "Who is it?" In addition, the wolf said, "It's mother."

But, the five little goats looked under the door and saw that his feet were brown, so it must be the wolf. So, the wolf tried again. He colored his feet white and said, "It's mother. I'm home. Open up."

The mother goat came by and saw the wolf trying to get in, so the mother kicked the wolf into the river. Now the five little goats were safe.

And, as for the wolf, he was all wet and soaked. He went home mad.

The Little Bunny and Two Little Sisters

Told by Rena, a third-grade student from Iran.

Once upon a time, there was a little bunny that had two little sisters. One day when their mother was going out to buy some bread, she said, "Be careful. Watch for the wolf!" "OK," they said.

So, their mother went. Then someone knocked on the door and the three little sisters said, "Who is it?" The wolf showed his hand. It was gray, not white like their mother's hand. The little sisters said, "We will not open the door!" This happened five times.

So the wolf went away. Later there was a knock at the door again and they said, "Who is it?" It was the wolf. He showed his hand again. This time it was white because he had covered it with flour. So, the little sisters opened the door. The wolf came in and ate two of them. The other one hid.

When the mom came back she saw only one kid, the one that hidden from the wolf. This one kid told the story of what had happened.

Then the mother and the kid looked for the wolf. When they found him they tore open the wolf's stomach and the two other bunnies came out. They all lived happily ever after.

The Brother, the Sister, and the Wolf

Told by Chul, a middle-school student from Korea.

Once there was a family with a brother and a sister. Every day the mother went to work to sell bread. She said to her children, "Don't open the door to anyone but me." They said, "OK."

One day she went to work, and when she was coming back, she met a wolf. Wolf told her if she gave him a piece of bread, he would not hurt her.

She gave him a piece of bread. This happened three times. The third time she did not have any bread, so the wolf ate the mother.

Then the wolf dressed up like the mother and went to the children's house. He said that he was their mother, but the brother said, "You are not our mother. Your voice doesn't sound like her." The wolf went away. The next time he ate an egg to make his voice sound softer. When he got there, they asked him to put his hand out and his arm to see if it was the mother's hand. They opened the door because the wolf had their mother's dress on with long sleeves.

When the wolf came in, he said he was very tired, and that they should go to sleep. So, they all lay down. The children then felt the wolf's arm and it was very hairy with scratchy hair, so they knew it was not their mother. They tried to run away. The wolf chased them. The children got back into bed and prayed for a rope. When a rope came down, they climbed up it to the sky and were safe. The wolf prayed for a rope, too. The wolf climbed up, but when he got kind of high, the rope fell down and down came the wolf.

The brother became the sun and the sister became the moon. But, because the sister was afraid of the dark, they changed places and the sister became the sun and the brother became the moon.

The Brahmin and the Goat

Told by Wali, a high-school student from India.

One day a Brahmin received a goat as a gift. He picked up the goat and set out for home, carrying it on his shoulders. Three rogues saw the Brahmin carrying the goat. They were hungry. They wished they could get the goat for a meal.

"That's a nice plump goat," said one of them. "Yes," said another, "It would make a good meal for the three of us. But, how can we get the goat? The Brahmin will not give it to us." "Listen," said the third rogue. "I have a plan." The third rogue then whispered into the ears of the other two. The other two rogues laughed. Then all three jumped up and hurried away.

The Brahmin walked on. Now, one of the rogues suddenly came along and stood in front of the Brahmin. "Oh, holy sir," said the rogue very politely, "why are you carrying that dog on your shoulders? Surely, to a Brahmin a dog is something unclean. I am surprised to see a Brahmin carrying a dog." "Dog?" shouted the Brahmin. "What are you talking about? Are you blind? This is a goat I have just received as a gift." "Now, don't be angry with me, sir," said the rogue in a calm voice. "I am only telling you what I see. But I'll say nothing more. Please pardon me sir." The rogue quickly went away.

The Brahmin walked on, muttering angrily to himself. A little further along the road the Brahmin met the second rogue. The second rogue looked at the goat and he looked at the Brahmin. "Oh, holy sir," said the second rogue in a sad voice, "you should not carry a dead calf on your shoulders. You know, it is disgraceful for a Brahmin to carry a dead animal." "Dead animal? Dead calf?" shouted the Brahmin. "What nonsense are you talking? Are you blind? Don't you know a live goat when you see one? This is a goat I have just received as a gift." "Please don't get angry with me, sir," replied the second rogue in a very humble voice. "Carry a calf, if you want to, a dead one or a living one. It does not matter to me. I'll say no more. Please yourself."

On walked the Brahmin. He felt a little worried. From time to time he glanced at the goat. It was a goat all right. But very soon he met the third rogue. "Pardon me, sir, " said the third rogue, "but I must tell you that what you are doing is most improper." "Improper?" asked the Brahmin. "What is improper?" "It is not proper, sir, for a holy man to carry a donkey. A Brahmin should not even touch such an unclean animal. You must know that yourself. Put it down, sir, before anyone else sees what you are doing."

The Brahmin was now puzzled. He was too worried to be angry. This was the third man he had met. And, each one had seen his goat as something different. First, it was a dog, then a dead calf, and now a donkey! Was this goat, then, a goblin or some sort of demon? Could it change itself every few minutes? Perhaps these men were right, after all. Greatly frightened, the Brahmin flung down the goat and ran home as fast as he could.

The rogue picked up the goat and hurried back to his friends. They were happy at the success of their plan. They had a goat meal.

The Wise Mother

Told by Sik, a middle-school student from Korea.

A long time ago, from our country, Korea, there was a custom named Go-ryo-jang. Go-ryo-jang was an old custom that many people believed in. They thought that when a person got old, you should leave them in a deep forest to die. When the old person died, someone would bury them. This was because during that time, the whole nation was in a very poor situation. There was hardly enough food for all the people who were not old. Also, some thought old people had no use. Time passed away, but this custom still did not disappear. No, it became even more strict during this period.

Once, during the time when the custom was very strict, there was a guy named "Park" and his old mother. Everyone looked up to him because of his great personality. He had a highly respected job from the government and the nation. But he wasn't happy because he knew his old mother was supposed to be sent to the forest to die.

It started a few days ago. He couldn't sleep. Even with his high respected job, he had to follow the custom Go-ryo-jang. Every citizen had to follow the custom of the country.

He kept thinking about what to do, but not one idea came out of his head. "There is no way I can do this to my mother. Even if I get in a lot of trouble I couldn't leave my living mother in the forest to die. "All right, then," he thought, "I'll hide her under the floor."

He immediately hid his mother under the floor. He told his family that he had followed Go-ryo-jang. He started to serve food to his mother privately. Because food was scarce, he took his own food to his mother.

"Mother, forgive me. There is no other choice. Please, I know it's hard, but try to be a little patient." His mother felt more sorry for her son than for herself because of all this trouble.

"Mother, don't worry, nobody knows. Don't worry and live a long, long time. I will tell the King, and put this ridiculous custom away."

"Thanks son, I'm happy. There is some light coming in here, and you always serve me food. But, I do worry about you. The last time someone tried to hide their parent didn't they get punished?"

Then, one day an ambassador came from a big country over the north river. That country had always been jealous of our country because it was expanding more and more. They would pick a quarrel. With any chance they would try to show that they were more powerful. But, every time they did so, our country would respond to them with brilliant ideas.

This time, the ambassador said something that caused the whole nation to shake.

He wanted to have a wisdom contest. We didn't know what kind of trap this might be. But, our country couldn't say no, because of the situation.

The ambassador showed everyone two horses that looked the same. He said arrogantly, "These horses are a mother and a daughter. You people are to figure out which is which, and you have 10 days to figure this out."

The King and all his servants were furious. Even Park was so worried his heart almost stopped. Both horses looked exactly the same. Even their eyes sparkled in the same way. They would never be able to guess which was which. The whole country began to panic. Whenever citizens met each other, they would talk about this. They were full of sighs. "We are in big trouble," they would say, "There is only one day left, and there is no one in this country who could possibly figure this out!"

The King sighed. He had a headache. His face looked as pale as it could possibly look. When Park saw this, he felt so bad that he thought his heart was going to be ripped apart.

Park came home with a face full of worry. When he went under the floor, his mother asked, "Is there any problem? You don't look so good."

"No mother," but he knew he couldn't fool his mother. So, he told her everything. After she heard the story, she looked like she was thinking. Then she smiled and whispered something into his ear.

When he heard what she said, her son's eyes got bigger. He was amazed at his mother's wisdom. It was miraculous.

Next day, in the royal palace, everyone looked at each other silently. The big country's ambassador said with an arrogant attitude, "This is the promised day, who will figure out the question?"

"I will." Park raced up. "I have a favor. Do you, ambassador, know which one is the mother?"

"Of course."

"Then write it down in a little piece of paper. You might argue it's not the right answer, even when I got the right answer."

"All right then."

When the ambassador agreed, Park asked a servant for some hay. Then, one horse came out and started to eat till he was full, then the other horse came out and started to eat. After Park saw this horse, he answered. "This horse is the mother. Even a horse lets her child eat first."

The Ambassador was surprised. He could only praise Park's wisdom.

Later, the King figured out that this wisdom came from Park's mother. Instead of punishing him for hiding his mother, he thanked him.

People then realized humans are useful and precious whether they are old or young. They started to talk about the privileges of a son. Soon the King banished the custom of Go-ryo-jang and amended the law to say that everyone should respect old parents.

The Shadow Story

Told by Sik, a middle-school student from Korea.

Once, a long time ago a man was tired from working hard. He was walking home and the sun was very hot. He came to a house with a big tree. The big tree made a big shadow. The tired man wanted very much to sit in that cool shadow, so he went to the house to talk to the owner.

"I want to sit in the shadow of your tree."

"You will have to buy it from me," said the owner.

"Buy the shadow?" asked the tired man. He thought about how cool it would feel to lie down in that shadow. So, he gave the owner some money.

Then he lay down in the shadow and enjoyed the coolness.

But, later in the day the shadow moved. The tired man moved, too. Now the shadow rested on the owner's house. The tired man went right into the owner's house. He was so anxious to stay with the shadow that he didn't even take his shoes off when he went into the house.

The owner's family wanted him out of the house. He wouldn't go.

They even wanted to buy the shadow back. He didn't want to sell it.

But, finally, he did sell it back to them for a lot more money than he paid for it.

A Stone in the Road

Told by Yegor, a middle-school student from Azerbaijan.

Once there was a village, and in this village there was a very rich man who had a big fine house. He was a very kind man. He always watched people passing by his house and often helped them. He would invite them to come sit in his house and to rest. He would give them food and drink.

But, this man was a little bit sad because everyone who passed by seemed lazy. None of the people looked like they wanted to work. So, he thought about this. Finally, he decided to order his servants to put a rock in the middle of the road right over a spot where he had put a pot of gold. Then he sat down and watched the people going by.

Soon a farmer came by and the farmer said, "Oh, look at this big rock in front of a rich man's house. If I were a rich man I would order my servants to take the rock out of the road!" And, he didn't even touch the stone. He just went away.

No one who came by touched the stone. They just said some words and then walked on. This made the rich man feel sad because no one tried to move the rock out of the way.

Much later, when it was getting a little bit dark, a little guy came by. He was coming from work and he was so tired. He saw the rock in the middle of the road and thought to himself, "Now it's getting dark out. Someone could bump into this rock fall down." So, even though he was tired, he moved the big rock out of the way. He could not believe his eyes when he found the big pot of gold!

At that moment, the rich man was looking and saw the little man take the pot of gold. The rich man was happy now because he found somebody who was not afraid of work, somebody who was kind, somebody who thought of others.

To Find a Wife

Told by Teresa, a second-grade student from Mexico.

Once there was a young man named Jose. He was looking for a wife.

When he was out walking one day, he stepped on an ant house and was surprised to hear a scream. It was an ant. He bent down and heard an ant say, "Hey, watch where you walk!" The young man was sorry he had stepped on the ant house so he built rocks around it so no one else could ever step on it again. The ant said, "Thanks."

As he went on his way, he passed a little lake. He heard a voice saying, "Help me." It was a fish trapped under a rock in the lake. He moved the rock and the fish swam free. The fish said, "Thanks."

He went on his way. As he was walking, he heard some squeaks. He looked down and saw two baby birds that fell out of their nest. He put them back in their nest. They said, "Thanks."

He went along his way and soon saw a castle. The king in this castle had a beautiful daughter. When the young man saw the king's daughter, he wanted to marry her.

The king said, "OK, but first you must do three things. One: you must pick up all these seeds." Then he took seeds and threw them out into the wind.

The young man thought he would never be able to find them all. But, then he heard a voice. He looked down and saw the same ant he helped. He heard a little voice say, "I will help you." The ant found the seeds for him.

Then the king dropped a ring into the lake and said, "Number two: you must return the princess's ring." The young man thought he would never find the ring in the lake. Just then, he saw the fish he had helped. In the fish's mouth was something shiny. It was the princess's ring.

Then the king took a necklace and tossed it high on to a tree. "Number three," said the king, "You must bring this necklace back to me."

It was up so high that the young man tried, but couldn't reach it. He was about to give up when the baby birds he had helped flew up there and brought the necklace to him.

So, the young man and the princess were married, and they
lived happily ever after.

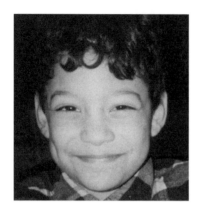

The Little Red Hen

Told by Lorenzo, a first-grade student from Mexico.

A little red hen tried to get some help to make some bread. She asked the donkey, and the cat and the dog. They all said, "No."

So, the hen had to make the bread by herself.

When the bread was ready, first came the donkey and asked for some bread, then the cat, and then the dog. But, the hen said "No" to the donkey and "No" the cat and "No" the dog.

Do you know why?

Because they did not help her!

The Lion and the Fox

Told by Yegor, a middle-school student from Azerbaijan.

Once there was a forest and in this forest, there lived different kinds of animals. The king of this place is a lion, you know.

Once, the lion went out to hunt. This lion was very kind to every animal. He did not eat healthy animals. He ate only sick ones that were going to die. He looked and looked, but he could not find anything. Then he found a fox, and he chased him. When he caught him and when he was ready to eat him, the fox said, "Don't eat me!" and those kinds of things. You know, a fox is kind of tricky. So, the lion said, "Okay."

So, he told the fox to come and live with him. When the lion caught something to eat, he brought it to the table and they both ate. Once, when this lion went hunting, somebody shot this lion. When he came home, he asked the fox for water. But, the fox took a big stone and threw it at the lion.

The lion said, "Why did you do this to me? I've been always good to you."

The fox said, "First when you came, you said, 'I have to kill you.' Now, I have to kill you!" So, he killed the lion.

This is the meaning of this story: in the world there are some people who, even though you are kind to them and everything, they will be bad to you. You cannot trust some people.

The Magpie and the Traveler

Told by Chul, a middle-school student from Korea.

One day a traveler was passing by, and he saw a big snake trying to eat a baby magpie. The traveler got his bow and arrow and shot the big snake. The big snake was dead.

When it got dark, the traveler did not have anywhere to sleep. In the woods, the traveler tried to find a house, but he couldn't find one. While he was looking, he saw a light in a house. He knocked on the door to see if there was anyone inside and a woman came out. The traveler asked, "Can I stay in your house for tonight? I don't have anywhere else to stay." She said, "Sure, but only I live in this big room. You must stay in another room." And she led him in to that room.

When it was almost midnight the traveler was not asleep. Something had opened the door. When the traveler turned around and looked there was a big, big, fat, long, and ugly snake. The snake said, "The big snake you killed with your bow and arrow was my husband. I'll do the same thing to you that you did to my husband." The traveler said, "Please don't eat me. I swear I didn't know." And then the snake said, "Well, if the big bell rings three times before I eat you in the morning, I'll let you live." The snake thought "Ha! I'm not as stupid as you."

The traveler could not sleep.

In the morning, the snake came into the room. The traveler closed his eyes and thought he was about to die.

Then the bell began to ring! It rang three times. The traveler and the snake were so surprised they both said, "Whaa! Whaa!"

The snake left silently.

The traveler went up the hill to where the bell was. He wanted to see who might have made the bell ring. When he reached the place, he saw a group of magpies dead on the ground. They must have died ringing the bell. The traveler buried all the magpies. He said, "You magpies were braver than me and I'll never forget that." And he left with tears in his eyes.

The Leopard's Tale

Told by Gwa, a first-grade student from Laos.

A mother leopard was fighting for people. She ate rabbits. She ate foxes. She did not eat people.

A hunter found the mother leopard. He shot her and killed her. He killed the mother leopard.

The hunter took it home. He made a coat out of its fur.

The baby leopards were still alive. Their father took care of them.

The hunter came out again to find the father leopard. The father leopard was brave. He growled at the hunter and the hunter ran away. But the father leopard ran after the hunter. He caught up with the hunter and killed him.

The babies grew up and became brave like their father. They had no more trouble with hunters.

They kept fighting for people like their mother did.

The Lion Story

Told by Yemi, a first-grade student from Somalia.

The lion was king. He killed all the people and said, "I'm king of the jungle!" He killed with his teeth.

The lion's brother and the queen were friends with all the people in Somalia.

"Get the people back alive," the queen said.

Then the king's brother killed the king, and he put his paws on the people's heart and they all came alive.

The king's baby became king. He was king of the jungle. After that they were friends with all the people in Somalia.

Not For You

Told by Consuela, a third-grade student from Colombia.

It was a very long time ago that this happened—a long time ago. My grandmother told me. Strangers came to Colombia who wanted gold. People in Colombia had gold then. But when the strangers asked for all the gold, the people did not want to give it to them. The people did not want to give it to them because the strangers were mean and bad to them. The strangers wanted all the gold for themselves.

The people decided to hide all the gold. Where to do it?

There was a beautiful lake in Colombia. It was a very deep lake. They took all the gold and threw it into the lake.

When the strangers came to get the gold, the people in Colombia said their gold had all disappeared. The strangers were angry, but they could do nothing. They looked everywhere and found no gold.

The gold was in the lake.

The gold is still in that lake.

Geck and the Bean Stem

Told by Zina, a middle-schooler and her brother, Boris, a third-grader from Bosnia. This is a compilation of the two tellings.

Once up on a time on a sunny day there lived a mom and her son. They lived in a small house. They were poor. One night, when they were cleaning some beans, they threw the bad ones out the window. When they woke up the next day, there was a bean stem with many beans. It grew up to the sky. Mom sent Geck to go up the bean stem to the sky. "If someone starts chasing you down the bean tree, I am going to dig a hole in the ground so you will fall into it. And now, go!"

The boy went up to the tree and climbed it up to the sky. When he got there, he saw a house in front of him. He went there and met a friendly mom giant and she told him that the dad giant was angry at everybody and that he was going to eat the boy if he saw him. The poor child hid, but when the giant came, he smelled him and started searching for him. After a long search, he found him. The boy started running and made it back down the tree and home.

The boy went back the next day. Instead of running when the giant started chasing him, the boy grabbed a chicken that laid golden eggs. He ran down the stem and told his mom to get an ax ready for him to use. The giant jumped down and fell into the hole that the boy's mother dug out. The mom and her son put dirt in the hole and covered the giant. The giant died. The boy took the ax and cut the bean stem down. The Mom and her son lived happily ever after.

Diamonds and Snakes

Told by Zina, a middle-school student from Bosnia.

Once there was a girl. Her mother died, and her father married again. Then he died. The girl had to live with her stepmother and stepsister. The stepmother thought she was prettier than her daughter, so she made her do all the dirty jobs. She made her clean and do everything.

Once she went to the well to get a pitcher of water. An old lady came there. She was a fairy godmother, but she was dressed like an old lady. The old lady asked for a drink of water, and the girl filled up the pitcher nicely and gave it to her to drink. The old lady was so glad that she thanked the girl. The old lady told the girl that when she talked, diamonds would come out of her mouth.

When the girl went home and started to talk, her stepmother saw all the diamonds coming out of her mouth. She got jealous, so she sent her daughter to the well. But her daughter didn't want to give the old lady anything to drink. So, the old lady said that when the daughter talked, she would have snakes come out of her mouth when she talked.

When the stepmother's daughter came back with snakes coming out of her mouth, the stepmother punished the girl with diamonds because she thought that girl had lied.

The girl who spoke with diamonds ran away to the woods. A prince saw her and thought she was pretty so they were married and lived happily ever after.

The Magic Apples

Told by Yegor, a middle-school student from Azerbaijan.

A long time ago, a king had three sons. In his garden, there was a magic apple tree. If you ate the apples from that tree, you would get younger. This king needed those apples.

One day one of those brothers saw that there were no apples on the tree. The brothers knew that somebody was stealing the apples. So, they decide that the older brother should stay on guard to see who was stealing. But, when he was on guard the older brother fell asleep. The middle brother did the same thing. When the younger brother stayed on guard, he cut his finger and put some salt on it. In this way, he would not sleep with his finger hurting.

In the dark after midnight, a big monster came to steal the apples. The younger son had put some mud under the tree so that when the monster walked away he would see the footsteps. He followed the footsteps and found a big cave with rooms in it. He saw that the monster had a girl there. When the younger son saw her, he fell in love with her. He killed this monster and freed the girl.

He took the magic apples from the monster, put them in his pocket for safekeeping and came home. When he told his brothers about it, they wanted to see the girl, so they went to the cave.

There was a well outside the cave. When they got there, the older brothers said they were thirsty and wanted some water. The younger brother said, "I'll go into the well and get you water." He got in the water, and when he started to come up, the older brothers cut the rope. The younger brother was stuck there a long time. He did not know what to do.

An old man came by and said, "Hey, son, what's your name?" And he said, "I'm [somebody—Alex, I think. I forgot his name]." The old man said, "There will be two ships coming to get you out of the well.

"Ships? I'm in a well! How can there be ships in a well? Where are ships?"

"Swim down to the bottom of the well," said the old man. "You will see it turns into a river. There you will see two ships—one black and one white. Get on the white one so you can go to the White World. Do not go with the black one. It goes to the Black World."

The younger brother jumped on the white one, but when he did, a big wave came up that threw him to the black one. The black ship took him to the Black World where everything is black. Everything is dark there. People wear black and people are crying and everything. He asked, "What happened?" They told him a big monster had taken all their drinking water. "The monster doesn't let drinking water come here." When the younger brother heard this, he found the monster and killed it. The king of the Black World asked him to come see him.

On the way, the younger brother saw a snake going up a tree to eat Eagle's babies. The younger brother killed this snake. The Eagle and the bird babies said, "Thanks. What can we do for you?" The younger brother was surprised that they could talk. He said, "Take me to the White World." The Eagle said, "I will, if you give me 40 pieces of meat and 40 pieces of water."

"Where can I find 40 pieces of meat and 40 pieces of water?"

"Go to the king of the Black World and ask for it."

When the younger brother got there, the king of the Black World was so pleased that he had killed the monster that he said, "You can marry my daughter for killing that monster."

The younger brother said, "No, I am in love with another. But, I would like 40 pieces of meat and 40 pieces of water."

The king of the Black World agreed.

Then the younger brother went back to the Eagle to ask for a ride to the White World. The Eagle said, "Climb on my back. When I say, 'Give me a piece of meat,' give me a piece of meat. When I say, Give me a piece of water,' give me a piece of water."

They flew off. The Eagle got meat and water when he asked for it—except for the last piece of meat. It fell down. So, there was no meat to give the Eagle. What to do?

The younger brother cut a piece of meat from his leg and gave it to the bird. When the bird tasted it, he knew this meat was different because it tasted so sweet. The Eagle didn't eat this meat, but put it under his tongueand held it there.

When they got to the White World, the Eagle flew down to let the younger brother off his back. But, he found that he could not walk on the leg where he had cut off a piece of meat. The Eagle took that meat from under his tongue and put it back on the brother's leg. Now he could walk. The brother said, "Thanks."

Then the Eagle gave the brother three feathers and said, "If you need me just send me one of these feathers." The brother said, "Thanks." Then, the Eagle flew away.

So, the younger brother looked around the White World and saw that everyone was happy here.

All this time he has kept the magic apples safe in his pocket.

When he got home, he saw that the older brother and the middle brother both wanted to marry the same girl that he wanted to marry. They fought about this.

The younger brother could see that he needed help. He blew one of the Eagle's feathers away to call the Eagle. The Eagle came and asked what the younger brother wanted.

"I want a suit of armor to fight my brothers for the girl." The Eagle gave him a suit of armor. When he put the suit on he fought his brothers and killed them.

When the girl saw him she remembered him and what he had done for her.

Then the king, his father, came. When the younger son took off his hat, the king saw that he was his youngest son. The king was very happy because his other sons had told him that a wolf killed the younger son. This was a lie.

The king was so happy to find his youngest son alive that he embraced him.

Now, his son took the apples out of his pocket and gave them to his father.

"My magic apples!" said the king as he embraced his son once more.

So, the king's youngest son and the girl got married and lived happily ever after.

The Angel Who Couldn't Fly

Told by Sik, a middle-school student from Korea.

Once an angel, a single guy, was down from heaven. He went to the woods when there was a full moon. He wanted to take a bath, so he took off his clothes. These clothes were full of flying magic. His special clothes had magic that made him able to fly.

When he was in the water, someone ran away with his clothes. It was a young woman who took his clothes and hid them. Now he was stuck because without his magic clothes he could not fly back to heaven.

He met this young woman and married her. Time went by. They had children and were happy. Even though the woman had hidden his flying clothes, her children found them. Of course, they tried them on, and when they did they flew up to heaven.

The children were sad because they missed their mother. A flying horse helped them. The flying horse came down and took their mother up to heaven to be with them.

The man was lonely without his wife and children. He prayed for a way up to heaven.

The flying horse could not come down for him because once, when the mother was making soup for dinner, she spilled hot soup on the horse, and the horse then ran away.

So the man prayed some more.

His family sent a bucket down from the sky. He got in the bucket and rode in it to heaven.

This angel and his family were happy together.

To Sing a Song

Told by Sik, a middle-school student from Korea.

Once there were twin brothers, one was good and one was bad. Each was born with an ugly growth on his face. This made life hard for them because often people teased them and called them names.

Their father said, "Do not let this sour your life. You are healthy and you are smart. You can show others how kindness can give you a full life."

The good brother became sad and quiet. When he did speak, he was kind and cheerful. He would sing a song to all who he met—those who called him names and those who did not. Because he had a beautiful voice, everyone who heard him smiled and thanked him for his song.

The bad brother became sad and quiet. When he did speak, he was mean and sullen. He would shout back ugly remarks to all who called him names. He even got into fights with people who did nothing to him but look at him strangely. He was angry all the time.

"Don't be so angry, son." their mother said to the bad brother. "Your brother has found something beautiful about himself—his voice. Perhaps you, too, can find something beautiful about yourself."

"I don't sing! And even so, I don't feel like singing!" said the bad brother.

Once, the good brother went into the woods to find firewood. When he had a big pile of wood, he wanted to go back home, but he did not know which way to go. He had wandered so far into the forest that now he was lost.

He put his load of wood down and sat under a big tree to think of what to do. As he sat, he began to sing. As always, his voice was beautiful. It was so beautiful that birds stopped their singing to listen.

Because he was thirsty, he went to a well nearby to drink. He sang another song as he drank. Then, accidentally, he dropped his ax into the well.

A Spirit came out of the well and asked, "Who is that singing?" When the good brother said he was singing, the Spirit wanted to know how he could sing so beautifully. "My mother says it's because of this growth on my face."

The Spirit showed the good brother a golden ax. He asked, "Is this your ax?" The good brother said, "No that golden ax is not mine." Then the spirit showed him a silver ax. "Is this your ax?" he asked. The good brother said, "No, that one is also not mine." Then the spirit showed him the ax that had fallen into the well. It was old and dingy. "Is this your ax?" he asked. "Yes. That is my ax." said the good brother.

The Spirit then removed the growth from his face.

The Spirit said, "Your beautiful voice comes from your goodness, not from the growth on your face. Anyone who sings so beautifully should have a beautiful face to go with it." The good brother reached up and touched his face. It was true! The growth on the good brother's face had disappeared!

When the good brother tried to thank him, the spirit only wanted to hear another song. And, it was true, the good brother could still sing beautifully. Then the spirit guided the good brother out of the forest. The good brother ran home singing for joy.

His brother was not happy to see that there was no growth on the good brother's face. He asked how it happened that now it was gone. When he heard about it, the bad brother set out to the woods to find the Spirit and to have his growth removed, too. He had never tried to sing, but he felt sure he could do it, if his brother could.

It was not long before he was deep in the woods. He found the well and dropped his ax into it. Then he sat down near the well and began to sing. But! Such a bad sound he made! His singing was just awful.

Soon the Spirit came saying, "Who is making that awful noise?"

The bad brother said, "Me. I am singing. Please remove my growth as you did for my brother."

"Just a minute," said the Spirit, "Is this your ax?" He showed the golden ax.

"Yes, yes!" lied the bad brother. "That is my golden ax."

"No, it is not!" said the Spirit. "First, you make awful singing sounds. Then you ask that I remove the growth from your face, and then you do not tell the truth. This is your ax." And, he showed the old, dingy ax that the bad brother had dropped into the well. "It's your badness that makes you sing so bad."

Instead of removing the bad brother's growth, the Spirit put another growth on his face! The bad brother now had two growths instead of one.

He tried to sing all the way home thinking that perhaps if he practiced, his singing would improve, and the Spirit would take the growths off his face. But, instead of singing, his voice sounded like groans and wails. The sounds he made kept getting worse and worse. People stuck their heads out of their windows holding their ears and saying, "Please, please stop that awful noise!"

When the bad brother got home, he stayed in the attic away from everyone. And, that's where he lived for the rest of his life.

But, the good brother lived a happy life singing and helping people.

No Room in the House

Told by Rena, a fourth-grade student from Iran.

Once upon a time, there was an old woman. She was very poor and she lived in a small house.

One day when it was raining very hard, the old woman was sewing and she had her fireplace on. As she was sewing, she heard a knock on the door. She said, "Who is it?" The cat said, "Mew, mew. It is me, the cat. May I sleep in your house tonight because of the rain and leave tomorrow morning?" The old lady was so kind that she gave the cat her bed to sleep on.

Then she started sewing again. In a few minutes, the doorbell rang. She said, "Who is it?" The sheep said to the woman, "It is I, the sheep. May I come and sleep? It is raining so hard. I'll leave tomorrow morning?" She gave the sheep a place, too.

Then more and more came until her whole house was full and she did not have any more room for herself.

She had to sleep outside.

Mohalam

Told by Rena, a fourth-grade student from Iran.

During the holiday called Mohalam, people in Iran remember. They remember by wearing only white or black. They remember a sad time when there was a war and the enemies were cruel. The people rode their horses into the desert where one of their enemies trapped them and kept them from having water.

The people were very thirsty, especially the children.

Three men tried to talk with this enemy. First, Amam Hassan went to them to ask for water for the children. "Please give us enough water for the children. They are suffering so." But, the enemy did not give him water. They shot him with arrows and killed him.

Then, Amam Hassaine tried to talk with this enemy. "Please give us enough water for the children. They are suffering so." But the enemy did not give him water. They shot him with arrows and killed him.

And then, Aman Ali tried to talk with this enemy. "Please give us enough water for the children. They are suffering so." Again the enemy did not give him water. They shot him with arrows and killed him.

Finally, a very brave woman, Fatima, went to talk to the other enemies who were in a nearby castle. She bravely made a speech to them and convinced them not to join in with the cruel enemy. They believed her and they broke away from the bad enemy. So, the children did have water.

And that's why we remember Mohalam.

A Fairy Tale

Told by Indira, a high-school student from India.

Once upon a time there lived an old widow with her two daughters. She was very poor and had hardly any money to spend for her house requirements. To run her house and her family she had to sew saris and sell them to her friends and neighbors. She stitched and repaired clothes of other people and also stitched and repaired clothes that other people gave her instead of paying her. Her daughters couldn't get an education because the schools were asking for too much money.

Next to this old widow-lady lived a rich and cruel lady. She was very mean to the widow-lady because she was poor. She also had two daughters who were just like her.

Once, an old beggar-lady was passing by the rich woman's house. She was hungry and asked the rich lady for some food. The rich lady lied, saying that she didn't have any food. She pushed the poor beggar back and threw her on the ground. Then the beggar lady went to the widow's house and asked for some food. The widow was so kind that she gave the beggar all the food that she had left. Seeing the widow's kindness and honesty, the beggar gave her a gift: to wish anything that she wants. But the old widow lady said, "I have everything, I don't want anything." The beggar wanted to give her a gift of her own choice, but since she didn't wish anything, she told her that whatever she did in the morning is what she will do for the rest of her life. Then the beggar left as if she were an angel who had come to give a gift to an old, poor, honest widow. Now the widow could make a living.

Next morning when she got up and started on her sewing, the first thing she did was open her closet and take out a sari. This process did not stop. It was probably the gift that the old lady had given her. She kept taking one sari after another out of the closet! The poor widow was surprised. Where did these saris come from? After a few hours she was tired, so her daughters helped her.

When this incident went into the ears of the rich lady, she was surprised, too. She went to her and asked who did this or how did this happen. The poor widow told her everything. Next day the beggar lady passed through that street again and when the rich lady saw her, she called her up and told her that she had some food today, if she would like to eat. The old lady went and ate whatever the rich lady gave. She made sweets and good other dishes. The old lady was surprised. After the old lady was done eating, she started to head out when the rich lady asked her to grant her the same gift that she granted the widow. Since she ate at the rich lady's house, she gave her the same gift: Whatever she did in the morning she would do the rest of her life.

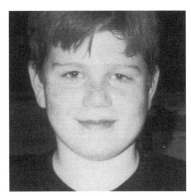

Next morning when she got up the mean, rich lady had only one thing in mind—that was to do something that would make her richer. She was about to get up from her bed when she accidentally spilled all the cotton out from her pillow and began sweeping it all up. As the old lady had said, whatever she did or touched is what she would do the rest of her life. So, she kept emptying her pillow cotton and sweeping it up. She could not stop. This process made her poor.

The kind and honest widow-lady became rich.

Little Red Riding Hood

Told by Zulfo, a third-grade student from Bosnia.

Once up on a time there was a little girl named Little Red Riding Hood. Her mom told her to take some cookies and biscuits in a basket to her grandmother. Along the way, she ran in to the woods and she picked flowers along the way to her grandmother. She got lost later, and a wolf came out and walked in front of her. The wolf asked, "Where are you going?" Little Red Riding Hood said, "I am going to my grandmother's house because she is feeling sick today. I am bringing her a gift with cookies, biscuits, and some flowers. But, I'm lost. I can't find my way to her house!" She cried.

The wolf said, "You can go up the hill there to the right and straight and you will be there. I will go this way and we will see each other up there, okay?"

Later the wolf came first to grandmother's house. Little Red Riding Hood was not there yet. He went inside to grandmother's bed, and he ate her. He put grandmother's clothes on and got inside the bed.

Later, Little Red Riding Hood got to the house. She knocked on the door. The wolf said, "Come in." Little Red Riding Hood came in. She looked at the bed and the wolf on the bed. She asked, "O, what big ears you have!"

The wolf said, "So I can hear you better, my dear."

"Oh, what big eyes you have!" said Little Red Riding Hood.

The wolf said, "So I can see you better, my dear."

"Oh, what big teeth you have!" said Little Red Riding Hood.

The wolf said, "So I can eat you!" He jumped up.

Just then a woodsman came by and cut up the wolf and took the grandmother out. Then he put rocks and balloons in his stomach and tied the wolf up. All the people celebrated.

REFERENCES

Aarne, A., and S. Thompson. 1973. *The Types of Folktales*. Helsinnki: Dellows Communications.

Adler, E. 2004. "Languages: Growing diversity presents challenges." *The Kansas City Star*, Sunday, September 26, 2004, 1 &8.

Allen, J. 2000. *Yellow Brick Roads. Shared and Guided Paths to Independent Reading 4–12*. Portland, Maine: Stenhouse.

Altwerger, B., et al. 1987. Whole Language: "What's New?" *The Reading Teacher*, 144–154.

Alvermann, D. 1986. "It's the Thought that Counts: Critical Reading in the Classroom." Paper read at 30th Annual Michigan Reading Association Conference, at Grand Rapids, MI.

American Folklore 2005. [Web site] [cited 2005]. Available from www.americanfolklore.net/folktales/hh.html-7k.

Anbar, A. 2004. *The Secret of natural Readers. How Preschool Children Learn to Read*. Westport, Connecticut: Praeger.

Applebee, A. N., J. A. Langer, and I. V. S. Mullis. 1988. *Learning to be Literate in America. Reading, Writing and Reasoning*. Princeton, NJ: Educational Testing Service.

Atwell, N. 1998. *In The Middle*. Portsmouth, NH: Heinemann.

Au, K. 1993. *Literacy Instruction in Multicultural Settings*. Orlando, FL: Harcourt Brace Jovanovich.

Au, W. 2004. "Left Behind?" *Rethinking Schools*, Fall.

Banks, J. A. 1988. *Multiethnic Education. Theory and Practice*. Newton, MA: Allyn and Bacon.

Barnes, D. 1975. *From Communication to Curriculum*. Hammondsworth, Middleses: Penguin.

Bauman, R., and A. Paredis. 1972. *Toward New Perspectives in Folklore*. Austin, TX: University of Texas Press.

Beresin, A. R. 1995. "Double Dutch and Double Cameras." *Children's Folklore: A Source Book*, edited by B. Sutton-Smith, J. Meechling, T. W. Johnson, and F. R. McMahon, eds. New York, NY: Garland Publishing.

Berlak, H. 2003. "The No Child Left Behind Act and Teaching Reading." Tempe, Arizona: Education Policy Studies Laboratory, Education Policy Research Unit. Arizona State University.

Bettelheim, B. 1976. *The Uses of Enchantment: The Meaning and Importance of Fairy Tales*. New York: Knopf. Distributed by Random House.

Blatt, G. 1993. *High Fantasies in Once Upon a Folktale*. Edited by G. Blatt. New York, New York: Teachers College Press.

Bligh, T. 1995. "Using Story Impressions to Improve Reading Comprehension." *Reading Horizons*, 287–229.

Bosma, B. 1992. *Fairy Tales, Fables, Legends, and Myths.* second ed. New York: Teachers College Press.

Bridging the Literacy Achievement Gap Grades 4-12. 2004. D. S. A. Strickland and E. Donna. eds., *Language and Literacy.* New York, N.Y.: Teachers College Press.

Brookline Teacher Research Seminar 2004. *Regarding Children's Words.* Edited by C. Ballenger. New York: Teachers College Press.

Brown, H. and B. Cambourne. 1990. *Read and Retell.* Portsmouth, NH: Heinemann.

Bruner, J. S. 1966. *Toward a Theory of Instruction.* Cambridge, MA: Belnap Press of Harvard University.

————. 1986. *Actual Minds, Possible Worlds*: Harvard University Press.

Brunvand, J. H. 1968. *The Study of American Folklore.* New York: Norton.

Bullock, A. 1975. *A Language for Life.* London: Her Majesty's Printers.

Burke, C. 1985. *Written Conversations in The Authoring Cycle: A Viewing Guide.* J. Harste, Pierce, K, Cairney, and T. Portsmouth, Series eds. N.H.: Heinemann.

Butler, F. 1977. *Sharing literature with children.* Prospect Heights, IL: Waveland Press.

Callahan, C. K. 1995. *Strategies to Facilitate Understanding in Classrooms with English Language Learners.*

Cambourne, B. 1988. *The Whole Story: Natural Learning and the Acquisition of Literacy in the Classroom.* Auckland, New Zealand: Scholastic.

Campbell, J. 1991. *Mythology: Primitive, Oriental, Creative, Occidental.* four vols, *The Masks of God.* New York: Penguin.

————. 1991. *Mythology: Primitive, Oriental, Creative, Occidental.* four vols, *Masks of God.* New York: Penguin.

Carney, S. 2005. *Folktales: What Are They?* [web site] 2005 [cited 2005]. Available from http://wwwfalcon.jmu.edu/ramseyil/tradecarney.htm.

Chandler, D. 1997. *Biases of the Ear and Eye.* 1997 [cited 1997]. Available from http://www.aber.ac.uk/-dgc/litoral.html.

Chou, N. 1986. *You Have to Live in Somebody Else's Country to Understand. Harmony in A World of Difference* Teacher/Student Study Guide: Anti-Defamation League of B'nai B'rith.

Claggett, F. and J. Brown. 1992. *Drawing Your Own Conclusions.* Portsmouth, NH: Boynton/Cook, Heinemann.

Clay, M. 1991. *Becoming Literate: The Construction of Inner Control.* Portsmouth, N.H: Heineman.

Coles, R. 1989. *The Call of Stories: Teaching and the Moral Imagination.* Boston: Houghton-Mifflin.

Conger, D., ed. 1987. *Many Lands Many stories.* Rutland, VT: Charles E. Tuttle.

de la Luz Reyes, M. 1992. "Challenging Veneralbe Assumptions: Literacy for Linguistically Diverse Students." *Harvard Educational Review.*, 427–446.

Delhalle-Ritzka, F. and Comstock, J. 2000. *Strategies to Help Facilitate Understanding in Classrooms with English Language Learners.* Kansas City, MO.

Delhalle-Ritzka.F. and J. F. Comstock. 1997. *Strategies to Help Facilitate Understanding in Classrooms with English Language Learners.* Kansas City, MO.

Dixon-Kraus, L. 1996. *Vygotsky in the Classroom.* White Plains, NY: Longman.

Doake, D. 1988. *Reading Begins at Birth.* Richmond Hill, Ontario: Scholastic.

Dueck, K. 1986. RAFT: Writing. *Kappa Delta Pi Record* 22: 64.

Dundes, A., ed. 1983. *Cinderella: A Casebook.* New York: Wildman Press.

Dyson, A. H. 2003. "The Brothers and Sisters Learn to Write, Popular Literacies in Childhood and School Cultures." D. Strickland and C. Genishi, eds. *Language and Literacy.* New York: Teachers College Press.

Eveld, E. M. 2004. "Karaoke: It helps students learn English." *Kansas City Star*: D1, D7.

———. 2004. "Teacher Uses Karaoke to Help Young Students Learn to Speak English." *The Kansas City, Star*, D1, D7.

Fernandez, R. 2001. *Imagining Literacy, Rhizomes of Knowledge in American Culture and Literature.* Austin, Texas: University of Texas Press.

Fitzgerald, J. 1995. "English as a Second Language Reading Instructiion in the US: A Research Review." *Journal of Reading Behavior.* 27: 115–152.

Franquiz, M. and M. de la Luz Reyes. 1998. "Creating Inclusive Learning Communities through English Language Arts: From Chanclas to Canicas." *Language Arts*, 211–270.

Freeman, Y. and D. Freeman. 1994. "Whole Language Learning and Teaching for Second Language Learners." *Reading Process and Practice, From Socio-Psycholinguistice to Whole Language*, C. Weaver, ed. Portsmouth, N.H.: Heinemann.

Freeman, Y. S. 1988. "Do Spanish Methods and Materials Reflect Current Understanding of the Reading Process?" *The Reading Teacher*, 654–664.

Freeman, Y. S. and D. E. Freeman. 1991. "Ten Tips for Monolingual Teachers of Bilingual Students. *The whole language catalogue*, K. Goodman, L. Bird, and Y. Goodman, eds. Chicago, IL: American School Publishers.

Freire, P. 1970. *Pedagogy of the Oppressed.* New York: Seabury Press.

———. 1985. *The Politics of Education.* South Hadley, MA: Bergin & Garvey.

———. 1987. *Literacy: Reading the Word and the Woprld.* South Hadley, MA: Bergin & Garvey.

Gandara, P. 1994. "The Impact of the Education Reform Movement on Limited English Proficient Students" *in Language and Learning.* Edited by B. McLeod. Albany, NY: State University of New York.

Garan, E. 2002. "Beyond Smoke and Mirrors, A Critique of the National Reading Project Report on Phonics." *How Ideology Trumped Evidence*, R. Allington, ed. Portsmouth, N.H.: Heinemann.

Garcia, G. E., A. I. Willis, and V. J. Harris. 1988. "Appropriating and Creating Space for Difference in Literacy Research." *Journal of Literacy Research*, 181–186.

Garcia, P. A. 2000. Preface. *Teaching Heritage Learners: Voices from the Classroom*, J. B. M. Webb, and B.L. Yonkers, eds. American Council on the Teaching of Foreign Languages.

Gardner, H. 1983. *Frames of Mind: The Theory of Multiple Intelligences.* New York: Basic.

Geertz, C. 1983. *Local Knowledge.* New York: Seabury.

George, R. 1985. "The Psychodynamics of Orality." *Orality & Literacy.*

Giroux, H. 1981. *Ideology, Culture & the Process of Schooling.* Philadelphia: Temple Un. Press.

Golden, J. M. 2000. *Storymaking in Elementary and Middle School Classrooms— Constructing & Interpreting Narrative Texts.* Hillsside, NJ: Laurence Erlbaum.

Goodman, K. S. 1982. *Language and Literacy: The Selected Writings of Kenneth S. Goodman.* F. V. Gollasch, ed. Boston: Routledge & Kegan Paul.

Goodman, K. S., et al. 1979. Reading in the Bilingual Classroom: Children Whose Language is a Stable Rural Dialect of English or a Language Other than English. Presented at Rosslyn, VA.

Gorman, R. 1972. *Discovering Piaget: A Guide for Teachers.* Columbus, Ohio: Charles E. Merrill.

Greene, M. 1995. *Releasing the Imagination: Essays on Education, the Arts, and Social Change.* San Francisco: Jossey-Bass.

Gregory, G. H. and L. Kuzmich. 2005. *Differentiated Literacy Strategies for Student Growth and Achievement in Grades 7-12.* Thousand Oaks, California: Corwin Press.

Gutstein, E. 2001. Math, Maps, and Misrepresentation. *Rethinking Schools* (Spring 2001):6-7.

Habermas, J. 1971. *Knowledge and Human Interest.* Boston: Beacon Press.

Halliday, M. A. K. 1975. *Learning How to Mean: Explorations in the Development of Language.* New York: Elsevier.

———, ed. 1984. "Three Aspects of Children's Language Development." *Oral & Written Language Development Research: Impact on Schools.* Y. M. Goodman, M. Haussler and D. Strickland, eds. Urbana, IL: National Council of Teachers of English.

Harste, J., D. Burke, and K. Short. 1988. *Creating Classrooms for Authors.* Portsmouth, NH: Heinemann.

Harste, J. l. 1984. "Examining Our Assumptions: A Transactional View of Literacy and Learning." *Research in the Teaching of English*, 84–108.

Hasan-Rokem, G., and D. Shulman. 1996. *Untying the Knot on Riddles and Other Enigmatic Modes.* New York: Oxford University Press.

Helbig, A. and A. R. Perkins. 1997. *Myths & Hero Tales: A Cross-cultural Guide to Literature for Children & Young Adults.* Westport, CT: Greenwood Press.

Hispanics' Schooling, *Risk Factors for Dropping Out and Barriers to Resuming Education.* 1994. United States General Accounting Office.

The History of Folktales 2005. [Web site] [cited 2005]. Available from http://www.geocities.com/athens/delphi/3603/contnetshtml.

Hoffman, C. 2001. *Mini-Digest of Education Statistics 2000.* Jessup, MD: National Center for Education Statistics. Office of Educational Research and Improvement. U.S. Department of Education.

Holdaway, D. 1979. *Foundations of Literacy.* Portsmouth, NH: Heinemann.

———. 1986. "A Natural Learning Model" *The Pursuit of Literacy.* Edited by M. R. Sampson. Dubuque, IA: Kendall Hunt.

Horneyansky, M. 1980. "The Truth of Fables." *Only Connect Readings on Children's Literature*, S. Egoff, G. T Stubbs, and L. F Ashley, eds. Toronto, Canada: Oxford University Press.

Igoa, C. 1995. *The Inner World of the Immigrant Child.* New York: St. Martin's Press.

Jacob, E. and C. Jordan. 1987. Explaining the School Performance of Minority Students. *Anthropology and Education Quarterly* 18 (4).

Jacobson, J. M. 1998. *Content Area Reading, Integration with the Language Arts.* Albany, NY: Delmar.

Jaynes, J. 1976. *The Origin of Consciousness in the Breakdown of the Biocameral Mind.* Boston: Houghton Mifflin.

Johns, J., S. Lenski, and R. Berghund. 2003. *Comprehension & vocabulary stratagies for primary grades*: Kendall/Hunt.

Johnson, G. 2000. Dept. of Human Development, Sprint Corporation. Kansas City, MO, 2000.

Jung. 1964. *Man and His Symbols*: Dell.

Klein, M. and F. Gale. 1987. "The Elusive Presence of the Word, an Interview with Walter Ong." *Composition Forum*, 65–85.

Krashen, S. K. 1981. *Second Language Acquisition and Second Language Learning.* Oxford: Pergamon Press.

———. 1982. *Principles and Practice in Second Language Acquisition.* New York: Pergamon Press.

———. 2002. More Smoke and Mirrors: "A Critique of the National Reading Project Report on Phonics." *How Ideology Trumped Evidence*, R. Allington, ed. Portsmouth, N. H.: Heinemann.

Kucer, S. B. 2001. *Dimensions of Literacy. A Conceptual Base for Teaching Reading and Writing in School Settings.* Mahwah, New Jersey: Lawrence Erlbaum Asso.

Lauritzen, C. and M. Jager. 1998. "The Transforming Power of Literature: An Afternoon in the Stacks." *The New Advocate*, 229–239.

Lindberg, B. 1988. "Teaching Literature: The Process Approach." *Journal of Reading*, 732–735.

Lloyd-Jones, R. 1977. "Primary Trait Scoring." *Evaluating Writing*, C. R. Cooper and O. Lee, eds. Urbana IL: National Council of Teachers of English.

Lourie, H. 1980. "Where is Fancy Bred?" *Only Connect: Readings on Children's Literature*, edited by S. Egoff, G. T. Stubbs, and L. F. Ashley, eds. Toronto, Canada: Oxford University.

Lynn, L. L. 1996. "Runes to Ward Off Sorrow: Rhetoric of the English Nursery Rhyme," *Only Connect: Readings on Children's Literature*, S. Egoff, G. Stubbs, R. Ashley, and W. Sutton, eds. Toronto: Oxford University Press.

Lynn, R. N. 1995. *Fantasy Literature for Children & Young Adults: An Anotated Bibliography.* New Providence, N.J.: Bowker.

Mahy, M. 1996. "A Dissolving Ghost," *Only Connect: Readings on Children's Literature*, edited by S. Egoff, G. Stubbs, R. Ashley, and W. Sutton, eds. Toronto: Oxford University Press.

Martin, R. 1992. *The Rough-Face Girl.* New York, NY: Putnam & Grosset.

Marzano, R. and E. Pickering. 2001. *Classroom Instruction That Works: Research-Based Strategies for Increasing Student Achievement.* Aurora, Cco: McREL.

Mathews, M. 1966. *Teaching to Read: Historically Considered.* Chicago: University of Chicago Press.

McGinley, W. and P. R. Denner. 1987. "Story Impressions; A Prereading/Writing Activity." *Journal of Reading*, 248–253.

McLaren, P. 1988. "Critical Pedagogy and the Politics of Literacy." *Harvard Educational Review*, 213–234.

McLaughlin, B. 1994. "First and Second Language Literacy in the Late Elementary Grades" *Language and Learning. Educating Linguistically Diverse Students.* B. McLeod, ed.. Albany, N.Y.: State University of New York Press.

McLuhan, M. and Q. Fiore. 1967. *The Medium is the Message.* Bantam Books.

Mead, G. H. 1934. *Mind, Self and Society.* Chicago: University of Chicago Press.

Meier, D. and G. Wood, eds. 2004. *Many Children Left Behind: How the No Child Left Behind Act is Damaging Our Children and Our Schools.* Edited by D. Meier and G. Wood. Boston: Beacon Press.

Merriam, S. 1998. *Qualitative Research and Case Study Applications in Education.* San Francisco: Jossey-Bass.

Moffett, J. 1992. *Teaching the Universe of Discourse.* Boston: Houghton Mifflin.

——— 1992. *A Child-Centered Language Arts Curriculum K–12.* Houghton Mifflin.

Myers, M. 1996. *Changing Our Minds: Negotiating English and Literacy.* Urbana, IL: National Council of Teachers of English.

No Letup in Unrest Over No Child Left Behind, July 7, 2004 [cited 2005] Available from http://www.teacherleaders.org/resources/nclb.html.

Norton, D. E. 1999. *Through the Eyes of a Child. An Introduction to Children's Literature*: Prentice-Hall.

OELA. 2005. The Department's Title III LEP Biennial Evaluation Report to Congress.

Ong, W. 1986. "Literacy and Orality in our Times." *Composition and Literature: Bridging the Gap.*, ed. W. B. Horner. Chicago: University of Chicago Press.

———. 1988. "Before Textuality: Orality and Interpretation." *Oral Tradition*, 259–269.

———. 1991. *Literacy and Orality.*: Cambridge Univeristy Press.

Pearson, P. D. 1997." The Politics of Reading Research and Practice." *The Council Chronicle, National Council of Teachers of English*, September, 1997.

Peregoy, S. F. and O. F. Boyle. 1993. *Reading, Writing & Learning in ESL: A Resource Book for K–12 Teachers*. White Plains, NY: Longman.

Raphael, T. E. 1982. Question-Answering Strategies for Children. *The Reading Teacher*, 186–190.

Rhodes, L. K. 1989. "Comprehension Instruction as Sharing and Extending." *The Reading Teacher*, 496–500.

Richmond, W. E., ed. 1957. *Studies in Folklore. In Honor of Distinguished Services of Professor Stith Thompson*. Bloomington, Indiana: Indiana University Press.

Rooth, A. B. 1951. *The Cinderella Cycle.* Lund: Gleerup, C. W. K.

Rosen, B. 1988. *And None of it was Nonsense: The Power of Storytelling in School.* Portsmouth, NH: Heinemann.

Rosenblatt, L. 1978. *The Reader, the Text and the Poem.* Carbondale, IL: Southern Illinois University Press.

———. 1983. *Literature as Exploration.* New York: Modern Language Association.

Routman, R. 1996. *Literacy at the Crossroads.* Portsmouth, NH: Heinemann.

Scribner, S. and M. Cole. 1978. "Literacy Without Schooling." *Harvard Educational Review*, November 1978.

Seigel, M. 1984. "Sketch to Stretch." *Reading, Writing and Caring*. O. Cochrane, et al., eds. New York: Richard C. Owen.

Shannon, P. and K. Goodman, eds. 1994. *Basal Readers: A Second Look.* Katonah, NY: Richard C. Owen.

Sleeter, C. 1994. "The Value of a Multicultural Education for All Students." *Language and Learning: Educating Lignuisticly Diverse Students*. B. McLeod ed. Albany, NY: State University of New York Press.

Smith, F. 1984. *Essays Into Literacy.* Exeter, NH: Heinemann Educational Books.

———. 1984. *Writing and the Writer.* New York: Holt Rinehart and Winston.

———. 1985. *Reading Without Nonsense*. NY.: Teachers College Press.

————. 1988. *Joining the Literacy Club*. Portsmouth, N. H.: Heinemann.

————. 1988. *Understanding Reading*. Hillsdale, NJ: Erlbaum.

————. 1990. *To Think*. New York: Teachers College Press.

Smith, M. W. and J. D. Wilhelm. 2002. "Reading Don't Fix No Chevys." *Literacy in the Lives of Young Men*. Portsmouth, NH: Heinemann.

Smith, N. B. 1965. *American Reading Instruction*. Newark, Delaware: International Reading Association.

Stories to Grow By 2005. [Web site] [cited 2005]. Available from http://www.storiestogrowby.com/.

Strickland, D. S. and D. E. Alvermann. 2004. "Bridging the Literacy Achievement Gap Grades 4–12." *Language and Literacy Series*, D. S. G. Strickland and C. Ganishi eds. New York, NY: Teachers College Press.

Sutherland, Z. and M. H. Arbuthnot. 1991. *Children and Books* (8th Ed.). New York: HarperCollins.

Sutton-Smith, B., J. Meechling, T. W. Johnson, and F. R. McMahon. 1995. *Children's Folklore: A Source Book*. New York, NY: Garland.

Takaki, R. 1993. *A Different Mirror*.: Little, Brown and Company.

Taylor, D. 1998. *Beginning to Read and the Spin Doctors of Science*. Urbana, IL: National Council of Teachers of English.

Tchudi, S. N. and M. C. Huerta. 1983. *Teaching Writing in the Content Areas: Middle School/Junior High*.: National Education Association of the United States. Distributed by the National Council of Teachers of English.

Thomas, J. 1996. "Woods and Castles, Towers and Huts: Aspects of Setting in the Fairy Tale." In *Only Connect, Readings on Children's Literature*, S. Egoff, G. T. Stubbs, and L. F. Ashley, eds. Toronto: Oxford University Press.

Travers, P. L. 1996. "Unknown Childhood." S. Egoff, G. Stubbs, R. Ashley, and W. Sutton, eds. Third ed, *Only Connect: Readings on Children's Literature*. Toronto: Oxford University Press.

Turner, S. R. 1994. *The Creative process: A Computer Model of Storytelling and Creativity*. Hillside, N.J.: Erlbaum.

Vogel, C. G. 1999. *Legends of Land Forms, Native American Lore and the Geology of the Land*. Brookfield, Ct: Millbrook Press.

Vygotsky, L. S., 1962. *Thought and Language*. Edited by E. V. Hanfmann and G. Vakar, eds. Cambridge, MA: Massachusetts Institute of Technology Press.

————— 1978. *Mind in Society: The Development of Higher Psychological Processes*. Edited by M. Cole, F. John-Steiner, and E. Souberman, eds. Cambridge, MA: Harvard University Press.

Watts-Taffe, S., and D. M. Truscott. 2000. "Using What We Know about Language and Literacy Development for ESL Students in the Mainstream Classroom." *Language Arts* 77 (3): 258–264.

Weaver, C. 1994. *Reading Process and Practice*. Portsmouth, NH: Heinemann.

Webb, J. B. and B. L. Miller, eds. 2000. *Teaching Heritage Learners: Voices from the Classroom*. Yonkers: American Council on the teaching of Foreign Languages.

Wendelin, K., H. 1991. "Students as story writers in the classroom." *Reading Horizons* 31:181-188.

Why the No Child Left Behind Act Will Fail Our Children. A fair Test Position Statement [cited 2005] Available from http://www.fairtest.org/nattest /bushtest.html.

Wrightson, P. 1996. "Deeper Than You Think." *Only Connect: Readings on Children's Literature*, edited by S. Egoff, G. Stubbs, R. Ashley and W. Sutton, eds. Toronto: Oxford University Press.

Zemach, M. 1977. *It could always be worse*. New York, NY: Farrar, Straus & Giroux.

Zipes, J. 1984. *The Trials and Tribulations of Little Red Riding Hood*. South Hadley, M: Bergin & Garvey.

INDEX

About the Author

Photo by Walt Whitaker.

RITA ROTH has forty years of teaching experience—half as a public school teacher and half as a teacher educator at the under-graduate and graduate levels. Recently retired as Associate Professor at Rockhurst University in Kansas City, she continues to work with teachers through staff development. Buidling literacy through competent, empowered teaching has been central to her work with prospective and experienced teachers. To Roth, nothing is more impressive than a classroom with pro-ductive teacher/student interaction. This level of teaching takes great skill and deserves much respect.

Literature—especially the folktale—forms the basis for Roth's research to advance literacy. Her work in collecting and retelling tales has proved effective on many levels. She completed the Bachelor's degree at the University of Pittsburgh, the Master's at Webster University in St. Louis and the Doctorate at Washingon University in St. Louis. Roth lives in Missouri with her husband. She has five children and five grandchildren.